1

Essential Portuguese Phrases

Phrases

Easy to Intermediate

Pocket Size Phrase Book for Travel

By

Fluency Pro

Disclaimer

Without the publisher's prior written consent, no portion of this publication may be reproduced, stored in a retrieval system, or transmitted in any form or by any means, electronic, mechanical, photocopying, recording, scanning, or otherwise, except as permitted under Sections 107 or 108 of the United States Copyright Act of 1976. Although every precaution has been taken in preparing this book, the publisher is not liable for any mistakes, omissions, or damages resulting from the use of the material included within. This book is intended solely for entertainment and educational purposes. The opinions presented are those of the author alone and should not be construed as professional advice or directives. The reader's activities are his or her own responsibility. The author and publisher take no responsibility or liability for the purchaser or reader of these contents. The reader is responsible for his or her own usage of any products or techniques referenced in this publication.

1600+ Essential Portuguese Phrases
First Edition: March 16, 2023
Copyright © 2023 Caliber Brands Inc.
Cover images licensed through Shutterstock.

Table of Contents

INTRODUCTION

Welcome! This book contains common phrases that will be very helpful when going to Portuguese-speaking nations, as they will assist you in communicating with people and doing daily tasks such as going out to eat and asking for directions. This book can also assist you in deciphering regional signage, and it may also improve your overall cultural awareness.

Portuguese is spoken as the primary language in Portugal, Brazil, Guinea-Bissau, Mozambique, São Tomé, East Timor and Angola. Certain communities in the United States, Canada, and Europe, as well as portions of Asia like Macau and Goa, also speak it. Moreover, Portuguese is recognized as a working language by the African Union, the European Union, and the Mercosur regional trading group.

The benefits of learning Portuguese are both personal and professional. It can provide professional chances in a range of industries, such as business, international relations, tourism, and teaching. Portuguese ranks well in terms of native language usage, with roughly 270 million speakers globally. By learning Portuguese, individuals are able to speak with a huge number of people from a variety of nations, which can be beneficial in the corporate world and beyond.

Cultural enrichment is an additional advantage of learning Portuguese. The literary, musical, artistic, and culinary traditions of Portuguese-speaking countries are extensive. Learning the language can facilitate access to these cultural elements and enhance one's appreciation for them. In addition, knowing Portuguese can make travel more fun and enlightening because it facilitates conversation with people and increases cultural awareness.

While going to Portuguese-speaking nations, a phrasebook can be a useful tool for communicating basic needs and navigating unfamiliar territory.

A phrasebook may include phrases for ordering food at a restaurant, seeking directions, and checking into a hotel, for instance. This can be very useful for those who do not speak Portuguese fluently, as it provides a quick and simple way to communicate with the native speakers.

In addition to providing translations, phrasebooks can also help individuals learn the basic grammar and sentence structures of Portuguese.

How This Book Is Organized

In this book, you will find over 1600 common Portuguese phrases organized by usage or situation.

Each entry provides the English phrase, the Portuguese translation, and a phonetic description in a uniform style. If you wish to know how printed Portuguese words sound, you can use the phonetic transcription to compare them to sounds you already know. Each transcription has been separated into syllables using dashes. Spaces separate the words. Capital letters accentuate syllables, but lowercase letters do not.

Vowels

Learning how to properly pronounce Portuguese vowels is essential. In the same way that English uses the vowels (a, e, i, o, and u), so does Portuguese. It is important to master the precise pronunciation of these vowels in order to communicate effectively in Portuguese, as they can sound different from their English and other language counterparts.

In Portuguese, the vowel "a" is pronounced like the English word "father," with an ah sound. The open vowel is a common first vowel for students to master. Vowel "e" sounds like "eh" in "bet" or "hey." Being a more compact sound than "a," it can be difficult for some students to separate from the vowel "i."

The I sounds more like the "ee" in "bee." This vowel is short and its high pitch sets it apart from the others. "o" is pronounced like "oh," as in "boat." The sound is airy and full, like the vowel "a." A "u" is pronounced as "oo," as in "food." The high-pitched, rounded tone might be difficult for some students to master.

It's important to remember that Portuguese vowels might sound different depending on the word, the speaker's accent, and the local dialect. Some Brazilian dialects may pronounce "e" as I while some Portuguese dialects may pronounce "u" as "o," to provide just two examples.

Vowels in Portuguese can be pronounced in a variety of ways because to the language's five basic vowels and a number of vowel combinations and diacritics (accent marks). As an illustration, the letter combination "o" is pronounced "ow" like in the word "now." The "é" diacritic is pronounced similarly to the letter "e," however with a little more contracted mouth. The diacritic ô is spoken like the letter o, but with a longer pause between sounds.

Learners of Portuguese can make great strides in the language and gain comfort and confidence while speaking with natives by paying close attention to vowel sounds and following the pronunciation standards.

Consonants

Portuguese consonants are pronounced in a similar way to English consonants, but there are some differences in pronunciation that learners should be aware of to communicate effectively in Portuguese.

Some consonant sounds are similar to English, such as "b," "d," "f," "l," "m," "n," "p," "s," "t," "v," and "z." These consonants are pronounced in a similar way to English, with some minor variations in the way some of the consonants are pronounced. For example, the "b" in Portuguese is pronounced like the English "b," but the "d" in Portuguese is pronounced like the English "d" in some words and like the English "j" in others.

There are also some consonant sounds in Portuguese that are not found in English, such as "ç," "ch," "j," "lh," "nh," "r," "rr," and "s" (in certain positions). The "ç" is pronounced like the "s" in "pleasure," while the "ch" is pronounced like the "sh" in "shoe." The "j" is pronounced like the "zh" in "azure," while the "lh" and "nh" sounds are pronounced like a "li" and "ni" sound, respectively, followed by a "y" sound. The "r" sound can vary depending on the dialect but is typically produced with a rolled or trilled "r" sound in Portuguese. The "rr" sound is a more intense version of the "r" sound, produced by rolling or trilling the tongue more vigorously. Finally, the "s" sound can be pronounced like the English "s" in some positions, but it can also be pronounced like the "sh" in "shoe" in others.

It is essential to pay attention to the pronunciation of consonants in Portuguese, as mispronouncing a consonant can lead to misunderstandings or difficulty in communicating effectively.

Stressors and Intonation

Stress and intonation play important roles in Portuguese as they do in many other languages. Understanding and using stress and intonation correctly is essential for effective communication and conveying meaning in spoken Portuguese.

In Portuguese, stress refers to the emphasis placed on certain syllables within a word. Unlike in English, where stress can be unpredictable and placed on any syllable, in Portuguese, stress is predictable and follows specific rules. In general, stress falls on the second-to-last syllable of a word, unless the word ends in "s," "l," "r," "x," or "n," in which case the stress falls on the last syllable. There are also a few other rules that determine where stress falls in certain types of words.

Using the correct stress in Portuguese is essential for conveying meaning and avoiding confusion. For example, the words "papá" (dad) and "papa" (potato) have different meanings but differ only in the position of stress.

Intonation, or the rise and fall of pitch in a sentence, is also important in Portuguese. Like in English, intonation can convey meaning and emotion in spoken Portuguese. Generally, the pitch rises at the end of a question and falls at the end of a statement. However, there are some variations in intonation patterns depending on the dialect and regional accent.

Intonation can also be used to convey emphasis, contrast, or surprise. For example, by placing emphasis on a particular word in a sentence, a speaker can draw attention to it and highlight its importance. In addition, by changing the intonation pattern in a sentence, a speaker can convey different shades of meaning or emotion.

ORDERING FOOD

Hi, table for two, please.
Oi, mesa para dois, por favor.
(oy, MEH-sah pah-rah DOIS, pohr fah-vohr.)

Could we have a booth/table, please?
Podemos ter uma cabine/mesa, por favor?
(poh-DEH-mohs TEHR OO-mah kah-BEE-neh/MEH-sah, pohr fah-VOHR?)

Can we see the wine list, please?
Podemos ver a lista de vinhos, por favor?
(poh-DEH-mohs vehr ah LEES-tah deh VEE-nyoos, pohr fah-VOHR?)

What do you recommend?
O que você recomenda?
(oh keh voh-SEH reh-koh-MEN-dah?)

Could we have some water, please?
Podemos ter água, por favor?
(poh-DEH-mohs TEHR AH-gwah, pohr fah-VOHR?)

I'd like to order the salmon, please.
Eu quero pedir o salmão, por favor.
(eh-oo KEH-roh peh-DEER oh sahl-MOWN, pohr fah-VOHR.)

Can I have the steak well-done, please?
Posso ter o bife bem passado, por favor?
(POH-soh TEHR oh BEE-feh behm pah-SAH-doo, pohr fah-VOHR?)

Could I get a side of fries with that?
Poderia trazer uma porção de batatas fritas junto?
(poh-deh-REE-ah TRAY-zeer OO-mah pohr-SAWN deh bah-TAH-tahs FREE-tahs JOON-toh?)

Could we have some more bread, please?
Podemos ter mais pão, por favor?
(poh-DEH-mohs TEHR mahys PAH-o, pohr fah-VOHR?)

Is it possible to make some substitutions?
É possível fazer algumas substituições?
*(EH poh-SEE-vehl FEH-zer ah-LGOO-mahs
soo-bee-stee-too-SAWN-ees?)*

I'm allergic to nuts, is there any dish without them?
Eu tenho alergia a frutos secos, há algum prato sem eles?
*(eh-oo TEH-noo ah-leh-RJEE-ah ah FROO-toos SEH-kohs, ah AHL-goom
PRAH-toh sehng E-les?)*

Could we have the check, please?
Podemos pedir a conta, por favor?
(poh-DEH-mohs peh-DEER ah KOHN-tah, pohr fah-VOHR?)

Can we pay separately, please?
Podemos pagar separadamente, por favor?
*(poh-DEH-mohs pah-GAHR seh-pah-rah-dah-MEHN-teh, pohr
fah-VOHR?)*

This was delicious!
Isto estava delicioso!
(EES-too EH-stah-VAH deh-lee-SEE-OH-soo!)

Do you have any vegetarian options?
Vocês têm opções vegetarianas?
(voh-SEHs TEH-ehm ohp-see-OHNS veh-jeh-tah-REE-ah-nahs?)

How spicy is this dish?
Quão apimentado está esse prato?
(kwow ah-pee-mehn-TAH-doo EHSS-eh PRAH-toh?)

Can I have a glass of red/white wine?
Posso pedir um copo de vinho tinto/branco?
*(POH-soh peh-DEER oom KOH-poh deh VEE-nyoh
TEEN-toh/BRAHN-koh?)*

Could we have some more napkins, please?
Podemos ter mais guardanapos, por favor?
(poh-DEH-mohs TEHR mahys gwahr-dah-NAH-pohs, pohr fah-VOHR?)

This is not what I ordered.
Isto não é o que eu pedi.
(EES-too NAWN EH oh keh EH-oo PEH-dee.)

Can you please heat this up?
Você pode esquentar isso, por favor?
(voh-SEH poh-deh ehs-kehN-TAHReh EE-soh, pohr fah-VOHR?)

Can we have the leftovers to go, please?
Podemos levar as sobras, por favor?
(poh-DEH-mohs LEH-vahr ahs SOH-bras, pohr fah-VOHR?)

Excuse me, is the service charge included?
Com licença, a taxa de serviço está incluída?
(kohm lee-SEHN-sah, ah TA-kah deh sehr-VEE-soh EHSS-tah in-kloo-EE-dah?)

Can we split the bill?
Podemos dividir a conta?
(poh-DEH-mohs dee-VEE-deer ah KOHN-tah?)

Can I get a to-go box for this?
Posso pedir uma embalagem para viagem para isso?
(POH-soh peh-DEER OO-mah ehm-bah-LAH-jehm pah-rah vee-A-jehm PAH-rah EE-soh?)

Is service included?
O serviço está incluso?
(oh sehr-VEE-soh EHSS-tah een-CLOO-soo?)

Can we have separate checks, please?
Podemos ter contas separadas, por favor?
(poh-DEH-mohs TEHR KOHN-tahs seh-pah-RAH-dahs, pohr fah-VOHR?)

Can we see the dessert menu, please?

Podemos ver o cardápio de sobremesas, por favor?

(poh-DEH-mohs vehr oo kahr-DAH-pioh deh soh-breh-MEH-sahs, pohr fah-VOHR?)

This dish is too salty.

Este prato está muito salgado.

(EH-steh PRAH-toh EHSS-tah MOO-ee-tooh sahl-GAH-doh.)

Do you have any vegetarian options?

Vocês têm opções vegetarianas?

(voh-SEHs TEH-ehm ohp-see-OHNS veh-jeh-tah-REE-ah-nahs?)

Thank you, the meal was great.

Obrigado(a), a refeição estava ótima.

(oh-bree-GAH-doo(a), ah reh-fey-SAWN eh-STAH-vah OH-tee-mah.)

BUYING TICKETS FOR TRAVEL

Insert the destination, where applicable

Hi, I'd like to buy a ticket to [destination], please.
Olá, gostaria de comprar um bilhete para [destination], por favor.
(oh-LAH, go-STAH-ree-ah de cohm-PRAR oom bee-YEH-tchee pah-rah [ ], por fah-VOR.)

How much is a one-way ticket to [destination]?
Quanto custa um bilhete só de ida para [destination]?
(KWAHN-too KOOSH-tah oom bee-YEH-tchee SOH de EE-dah pah-rah [ ]?)

Do you have any discounts for students/seniors/military?
Vocês têm descontos para estudantes/idosos/militares?
(vo-SEHZ teh-um des-KOHN-tohs pah-rah es-too-DAN-tehz/ee-DOH-sohs/mee-lee-TAH-rehz?)

Can I buy a round-trip ticket to [destination]?
Posso comprar um bilhete de ida e volta para [destination]?
(POH-soh cohm-PRAR oom bee-YEH-tchee de EE-dah ee VOHL-tah pah-rah [ ]?)

Are there any direct flights to [destination]?
Existem voos diretos para [destination]?
(eh-shee-STEM voos dee-REH-tohs pah-rah [ ]?)

Can I reserve a seat on this flight/train?
Posso reservar um assento neste voo/trem?
(POH-soh reh-zehr-VAHR oom ah-SEHN-too NEH-stee voh/trehm?)

What's the next available flight/train to [destination]?
Qual é o próximo voo/trem disponível para [destination]?
(kwahl eh oh PROH-ksee-moh voh/trehm dis-poh-NEE-vehl pah-rah []?)

Is there a layover on this flight?
Há escala neste voo?
(AH es-KAH-lah NEH-stee voh?)

How long is the layover?
Quanto tempo dura a escala?
(KWAHN-too TEHM-poh DOO-rah ah es-KAH-lah?)

Can I choose my seat on this flight?
Posso escolher meu assento neste voo?
(POH-soh ehs-kohl-YEH-oor may-oo ah-SEHN-too NEH-stee voh?)

What's the earliest flight/train to [destination]?
Qual é o primeiro voo/trem para [destination]?
(kwahl eh oh PRYEY-roh voh/trehm pah-rah [ ]?)

Can I change my flight/train schedule?
Posso mudar meu horário de voo/trem?
(POH-soh moo-DAHR may-oo oh-RAH-ree-oh de voh/trehm?)

What's the latest flight/train to [destination]?
Qual é o último voo/trem para [destination]?
(kwahl eh oh OOL-tee-moh voh/trehm pah-rah [ ]?)

How long is the flight/train to [destination]?
Quanto tempo dura o voo/trem para [destination]?
(KWAHN-too TEHM-poh DOO-rah oh voh/trehm pah-rah [ ]?)

Is there a refund policy if I can't make my flight/train?
Há uma política de reembolso se eu não puder pegar meu voo/trem?
(AH OO-mah po-lih-SEE-ah deh reh-eem-BOHL-soo seh eh-oo NAH-o poo-DEHR peh-gahr may-oo voh/trehm?)

Can I pay with a credit card/cash?
Posso pagar com cartão de crédito/dinheiro?
(POH-soh pah-GAHR kohm kahr-TAH-oh deh KREH-dee-toh/dee-NHEY-roo?)

Do I need to show ID to purchase a ticket?
Preciso mostrar identificação para comprar um bilhete?
(preh-SEE-doh moh-STRAHR ee-den-tee-fee-kah-see-OHN pah-rah cohm-PRAR oom bee-YEH-tchee?)

Can I get a receipt for my ticket?
Posso receber um recibo para meu bilhete?
(POH-soh reh-SEH-behr oom reh-SEE-boo pah-rah may-oo bee-YEH-tchee?)

How many bags can I bring on the flight/train?
Quantas malas eu posso trazer no voo/trem?
(KWAN-tahs MAH-lahs eh-oo POH-soh TREE-zehr no voh/trehm?)

Is there an extra fee for baggage?
Há uma taxa extra para bagagem?
(AH OO-mah TAX-ah EHKS-trah pah-rah bah-GAH-jehm?)

Can I check in online?
Posso fazer check-in online?
(POH-soh fah-ZEHR check-in online?)

Can I choose my seat when checking in?
Posso escolher meu assento ao fazer check-in?
(POH-soh ehs-kohl-YEH-oor may-oo ah-SEHN-too ah-oo fah-ZEHR check-in?)

How early should I arrive for my flight/train?
Com quantos minutos de antecedência devo chegar para o meu voo/trem?
(kohm KWAHN-tohs mee-NOO-tohs deh ahn-teh-seh-DEN-see-ah DEH-voh cheh-GAHR pah-rah oh may-oo voh/trehm?)

Can I bring a pet on the flight/train?
Posso trazer um animal de estimação no voo/trem?
(POH-soh TREE-zehr oom ah-nee-MAHL deh eh-stee-mah-SAHW no voh/trehm?)

Is there a special section for families with children?
Há uma área especial para famílias com crianças?
(AH OO-mah AH-ree-ah eh-speh-SEE-ahl pah-rah fah-MEE-lee-ahs kohm kree-AHN-sahs?)

Is there a vegetarian option for meals on the flight/train?
Há uma opção vegetariana para as refeições no voo/trem?
(AH OO-mah oh-PSHAWN veh-geh-tah-ree-AH-nah pah-rah ahs reh-feh-ee-SHAWN no voh/trehm?)

Can I request a special meal?
Posso solicitar uma refeição especial?
(POH-soh soh-lee-see-TAHR oom-ah reh-feh-ee-SHAWN eh-speh-SEE-ahl?)

What is the maximum weight for baggage?
Qual é o peso máximo para bagagem?
(kwahl eh oh PEH-soo MAH-ks-ee-moh pah-rah bah-GAH-jehm?)

Can I upgrade my seat/class?
Posso atualizar meu assento/classe?
(POH-soh ah-too-ah-lee-ZAHHR may-oo ah-SEHN-too/klah-SEE?)

Is there Wi-Fi on the flight/train?
Há Wi-Fi no voo/trem?
(AH OO-mah WEE-fee noh voh/trehm?)

STATE OF EMERGENCY

Help!
Ajuda!
(ah-JOO-dah)

Call 911!
Ligue para o 911!
(LEE-gwe pah-rah oh noh-veh-zeh-ee-um)

I need immediate assistance.
Eu preciso de assistência imediata.
(ay-oo preh-SEE-soh jee ah-sis-TEN-see-ah ee-meh-dee-AH-tah)

Someone call an ambulance!
Alguém chame uma ambulância!
(ahl-GHEM sha-mee OO-mah ahm-boo-LAHN-see-ah)

This is an emergency!
Isto é uma emergência!
(ees-TOH eh OO-mah eh-mer-JHEN-see-ah)

Please help me!
Por favor, ajude-me!
(por fah-VOHR, ah-JOO-deh meh)

I'm in trouble!
Estou em apuros!
(ehs-TOH ehm ah-POO-roos)

I'm in danger!
Estou em perigo!
(ehs-TOH ehm peh-REE-goh)

I'm hurt!
Eu estou ferido!
(ay-oo eh-STOH feh-REE-doh)

I'm injured!
Eu estou machucado!
(ay-oo eh-STOH mah-SHOO-kah-doh)

I'm bleeding!
Eu estou sangrando!
(ay-oo eh-STOH sahng-GRAHN-doh)

I can't breathe!
Eu não consigo respirar!
(ay-oo nahw kohn-SEE-goh reh-spee-RAHR)

Please call for help!
Por favor, chame ajuda!
(por fah-VOHR, SHAH-meh ah-JOO-dah)

Somebody please help me!
Alguém, por favor, me ajude!
(ahl-GHEM, por fah-VOHR, meh ah-JOO-deh)

I'm having a heart attack!
Estou tendo um ataque cardíaco!
(ehs-TOH TEHN-doh oom ah-TAH-keh kahr-DEE-ah-koh)

I'm having a stroke!
Estou tendo um derrame!
(ehs-TOH TEHN-doh oom deh-RAH-meh)

I'm having an allergic reaction!
Estou tendo uma reação alérgica!
(ehs-TOH TEHN-doh OO-mah reh-ah-SOWNGH ah-LEHR-jee-kah)

I'm having a seizure!
Estou tendo uma convulsão!
(ehs-TOH TEHN-doh OO-mah kohn-vool-SOWNGH)

I'm choking!
Estou engasgando!
(ehs-TOH ehn-gahs-GAHN-doh)

I'm drowning!
Estou me afogando!
(ehs-TOH meh ah-foh-GAHN-doh)

My house is on fire!
Minha casa está pegando fogo!
(MEE-nya KAH-sah ehs-TAH peh-GAHN-doh FOH-goh)

My car crashed!
Meu carro bateu!
(MEH-ooh KAH-roo bah-TEH-oo)

My child is missing!
Meu filho está desaparecido!
(MEH-ooh FEE-lyoh eh-STAH deh-sah-pah-REH-see-doh)

My loved one is in danger!
Meu ente querido está em perigo!
(MEH-ooh EN-teh keh-REE-doh eh-STAH ehm peh-REE-goh)

I need medical attention!
Eu preciso de atenção médica!
(ay-oo preh-SEE-soh deh ah-ten-SEE-own MEH-dee-kah)

I'm trapped!
Estou preso!
(ehs-TOH PREH-soh)

I'm lost!
Estou perdido!
(ehs-TOH pehr-DEE-doh)

I'm stranded!
Estou encalhado!
(ehs-TOH ehn-kah-LHAH-doh)

My pet needs urgent medical care!
Meu animal de estimação precisa de cuidados médicos urgentes!
(MEH-ooh ah-nee-MAHL deh eh-STEE-mah-SOWNGH PREH-see-sah deh kwee-DAH-dohs MEH-dee-kohs oor-ZHEN-tis)

I need the police!
Eu preciso da polícia!
(ay-oo preh-SEE-soh dah poh-LEE-see-ah)

TECH SUPPORT

I am having problems with my computer.
Eu estou tendo problemas com meu computador.
(ehoo eh-STOH TEHN-doh proh-BLEH-mahs kohm MEH-oo kohm-poo-tah-DOR.)

My internet connection is slow.
Minha conexão com a internet está lenta.
(MEE-nya kon-eks-SAHW kohm ah een-teh-nehT EH-stah LEN-tah.)

I forgot my password.
Eu esqueci minha senha.
(ehoo ess-KEH-see MEE-nya SEHN-yah.)

The website is not loading.
O site não está carregando.
(oh SEE-tee neh-oh EHSS-tah kah-reh-GAHN-doo.)

My email account is not working.
Minha conta de e-mail não está funcionando.
(MEE-nya KOHN-tah deh ee-MAYL neh-oh EHSS-tah foo-see-oh-nahn-DOO.)

The printer is not printing.
A impressora não está imprimindo.
(ah eem-PREH-soh-rah neh-oh EHSS-tah eem-PREE-meen-doo.)

My computer crashed.
Meu computador travou.
(MEH-oo kohm-poo-tah-DOR trah-VOH.)

The software is not working.
O software não está funcionando.
(oh sohf-TWAA-reh neh-oh EHSS-tah foo-see-oh-nahn-DOO.)

I am receiving error messages.
Estou recebendo mensagens de erro.
(eh-STOH reh-seh-BEHN-doo mehn-SAH-jehns deh EH-roo.)

The computer is frozen.
O computador está travado.
(oh kohm-poo-tah-DOR EH-stah trah-VOH-doo.)

My keyboard is not working.
Meu teclado não está funcionando.
(MEH-oo teh-KLAH-doo neh-oh EHSS-tah foo-see-oh-nahn-DOO.)

I cannot access my files.
Não consigo acessar meus arquivos.
(nah-oh kohn-SEE-goh ah-seh-SAR meh-ooss ah-r-kee-vohs.)

The computer is making strange noises.
O computador está fazendo barulhos estranhos.
(oh kohm-poo-tah-DOR EH-stah fah-ZEHN-doo bah-roo-lyoosh ehs-TRAHN-yoosh.)

I need to update my software.
Preciso atualizar meu software.
(preh-SEE-doh ah-too-ah-lee-ZAHR MEH-oo sohf-TWAA-reh.)

My computer is infected with a virus.
Meu computador está infectado com um vírus.
(MEH-oo kohm-poo-tah-DOR EH-stah een-fehk-TAH-doo kohm oong VEE-roos.)

The mouse is not working.
O mouse não está funcionando.
(oh MOH-zee neh-oh EHSS-tah foo-see-oh-nahn-DOO.)

I accidentally deleted important files.
Eu deletei acidentalmente arquivos importantes.
(ehoo deh-lee-TEH-ee ah-see-den-tahl-MEHN-tee ah-r-kee-vohs eem-pohr-TAHN-tees.)

I need help setting up my new device.

Eu preciso de ajuda para configurar meu novo dispositivo.

(ehoo preh-SEE-soh deh ah-JOO-dah pah-rah kohn-fee-goo-RAHR MEH-oo NOH-voh dee-see-pee-ti-voh.)

The screen is black.

A tela está preta.

(ah TEH-lah EH-stah PREH-tah.)

I accidentally spilled water on my laptop.

Eu derramei água acidentalmente no meu laptop.

(ehoo deh-rah-MEH-ee AHG-wah ah-see-den-tahl-MEHN-tee no MEH-oo LAHP-tohp.)

The battery is not charging.

A bateria não está carregando.

(ah bah-teh-REE-ah neh-oh EHSS-tah kah-reh-GAHN-doo.)

My computer is overheating.

Meu computador está superaquecendo.

(MEH-oo kohm-poo-tah-DOR EH-stah soo-pehr-ah-keh-CEN-doo.)

The sound is not working.

O som não está funcionando.

(oh sohm neh-oh EHSS-tah foo-see-oh-nahn-DOO.)

I accidentally uninstalled an important program.

Eu desinstalei acidentalmente um programa importante.

(ehoo deh-seens-tah-LEH-ee ah-see-den-tahl-MEHN-tee oong proh-grah-mah eem-pohr-TAHN-tee.)

The internet is not connecting.

A internet não está conectando.

(ah een-teh-nehT neh-oh EHSS-tah kohn-ehk-TAHN-doo.)

I need to recover deleted files.

Eu preciso recuperar arquivos deletados.

(ehoo preh-SEE-soh reh-koo-peh-RAHR ah-ree-kee-vohs deh-lee-TAH-dohs.)

My printer is not printing.
Minha impressora não está imprimindo.
(MEE-nya eem-PREH-soh-rah neh-oh EHSS-tah eem-PREEN-deeN-doo.)

I can't access my email.
Eu não consigo acessar meu email.
(ehoo neh-oh kohn-SEE-goh ah-kess-AHR MEH-oo ih-mehl.)

I forgot my password.
Eu esqueci minha senha.
(ehoo ess-KEH-see MEE-nya SEH-nyah.)

The CD/DVD drive is not working.
A unidade de CD/DVD não está funcionando.
*(ah oo-nee-DAH-deh deh see-deh-DEH-vee-DEH neh-oh EHSS-tah
foo-see-oh-nahn-DOO.)*

SMALL TALK

How's it going?
Como vai?
(KOH-moh VAI?)

What have you been up to lately?
O que tens feito ultimamente?
(oh keh tens FAY-toh ool-tee-MAHN-teh?)

How was your weekend?
Como foi o teu fim de semana?
(KOH-moh FOI oh TEH-oo feem deh seh-MAHN?)

Did you catch the game last night?
Viste o jogo de ontem à noite?
(VEES-teh oh JOH-goh deh ohn-TEM ah NOY-teh?)

What do you like to do in your free time?
O que gostas de fazer no teu tempo livre?
(oh keh GOH-stahsh deh fah-ZEHR noh TEH-oo TEHM-poo LEE-vreh?)

Have you seen any good movies or TV shows lately?
Tens visto bons filmes ou séries de TV ultimamente?
*(tens VEE-stoh bohns FEE-lehms oh SEH-ree-ehsh deh TV
ool-tee-MAHN-teh?)*

How's work/school going?
Como vai o trabalho/a escola?
(KOH-moh VAI oh trah-BAH-lyoo/ah es-KOH-lah?)

Do you have any plans for the weekend?
Tens planos para o fim de semana?
(tens PLAH-nohsh PAH-rah oh feem deh seh-MAHN?)

What's new with you?
O que há de novo contigo?
(oh keh ah deh NO-vo KOHN-tee-goh?)

How's the family doing?
Como está a família?
(KOH-moh es-TAH ah fah-MEE-lyah?)

What kind of music do you like?
Que tipo de música gostas?
(keh TEE-poh deh MOO-zee-kah GOH-stahsh?)

Have you tried any new restaurants lately?
Tens experimentado algum restaurante novo ultimamente?
(tens es-peh-ree-men-TAH-doh ahl-goom rehs-taw-RAHN-teh NO-vo ool-tee-MAHN-teh?)

What's your favorite hobby?
Qual é o teu hobby favorito?
(KWAL eh oh TEH-oo HO-bee fah-voh-REE-toh?)

Are you originally from around here?
És daqui originalmente?
(ehsh dah-KEE oh-ree-jee-nahl-MEN-teh?)

What do you think about the weather today?
O que achas do tempo hoje?
(oh keh AH-shash doh TEHM-poh OH-zhee?)

Do you like to travel? Where have you been?
Gostas de viajar? Onde tens estado?
(GOH-stahsh deh VEE-ah-jahr? OWN-deh tens es-TAH-doh?)

How do you like to spend your vacations?
Como gostas de passar as tuas férias?
(KOH-moh GOH-stahsh deh pah-SAHR ahs TOO-ash FAY-ree-ahsh?)

Do you like to read? What's your favorite book?
Gostas de ler? Qual é o teu livro favorito?
(GOH-stahsh deh LEHR? KWAL eh oh TEH-oo LEE-vroh fah-voh-REE-toh?)

What kind of sports do you like to watch/play?
Que tipo de desportos gostas de ver/jogar?
(keh TEE-poh deh des-POHR-toosh GOH-stahsh deh VEHR/JOH-gahr?)

Do you have any favorite TV shows?
Tens alguma série de TV favorita?
(tens ahl-GOO-mah SEH-ree-eh deh TV fah-voh-REE-tah?)

What do you do for exercise?
O que fazes para exercitar-te?
(oh keh FAH-zesh PAH-rah ehk-sehr-SEE-tahr-teh?)

Do you have any siblings?
Tens irmãos/irmãs?
(tens eer-MAH-oosh/ eer-MAH-sh?)

How did you get interested in your job/profession?
Como te interessaste pelo teu trabalho/profissão?
(KOH-moh teh in-teh-ress-TAHSH-teh PEH-loh TEH-oo trah-BAH-lyoo/proh-fee-SAWNG?)

Do you like to cook?
Gostas de cozinhar?
(GOH-stahsh deh koh-zee-NYAHHR?)

What's your favorite kind of food?
Qual é o teu tipo de comida favorito?
(KWAL eh oh TEH-oo TEE-poh deh koh-MEE-dah fah-voh-REE-toh?)

Do you have any favorite places to visit?
Tens algum lugar favorito para visitar?
(tens ahl-goom loo-GAHR fah-voh-REE-toh PAH-rah vee-zee-TAHR?)

What's your favorite season?
Qual é a tua estação do ano favorita?
(KWAL eh ah TOO-ah ehs-tah-SAWNG doh ahn-yoo fah-voh-REE-tah?)

What's your favorite holiday?
Qual é o teu feriado favorito?
(KWAL eh oh TEH-oo fay-REE-ah-doo fah-voh-REE-toh?)

Do you have any upcoming plans or events to look forward to?
Tens planos ou eventos para os quais estás ansioso/a?
(tens PLAH-noosh oh-oo eh-VEHN-toosh PAH-rah oosh KOYSH es-TAHS ahn-SEE-oh-soh/ah?)

What kind of music do you like to listen to?
Que tipo de música gostas de ouvir?
(keh TEE-poh deh MOO-zee-kah GOH-stahsh deh oh-VEER?)

DATING

Hi, it's great to finally meet you!
Olá, é ótimo finalmente te conhecer!
(oh-LAH, eh OH-tee-moh fin-al-MEN-tee chee co-ney-SEHR)

How's your day been so far?
Como tem sido o seu dia até agora?
(KOH-moh tehm SEE-doh ooh seh-oo DEE-ah a-teh A-goh-rah)

Would you like a drink?
Você gostaria de uma bebida?
(vo-SEH gos-tee-ah-REE-ah jee ooh-mah beh-BEE-dah)

What do you do for fun?
O que você faz para se divertir?
(oh keh vo-SEH fahz pah-rah see dee-vehr-TEER)

Tell me about yourself.
Fale sobre você mesmo.
(FAH-leh soh-breh vo-SEH mehss-moh)

So, where are you from originally?
Então, de onde você é originalmente?
(EN-taum, jee OHN-deh vo-SEH eh oh-ree-jee-nahl-MEN-tee)

What kind of music do you like?
Que tipo de música você gosta?
(keh TEE-poh jee MOO-zee-kah vo-SEH gos-tah)

Have you traveled anywhere interesting lately?
Você viajou para algum lugar interessante recentemente?
*(vo-SEH vee-ah-JOH-oo pah-rah ahl-goom LOO-gahr
een-teh-ress-SAHN-tee heh-SEN-teh-mehn-tee)*

What do you like to do in your free time?
O que você gosta de fazer no seu tempo livre?
(oh keh vo-SEH gos-tah jee fah-ZEHR noh seh-oo TEHM-poh LEE-vreh)

This place is really nice, don't you think?
Este lugar é realmente legal, você não acha?
(EH-steh LOO-gahr eh reh-ahl-men-tee lee-GAHL, vo-SEH naum AH-shah)

So, how did you get into your line of work?
Então, como você entrou na sua área de trabalho?
(EN-taum, KOH-moh vo-SEH en-TROH-oo nah soo-ah AH-reh-ah jee trah-BAH-lyoo)

What's your favorite movie?
Qual é o seu filme favorito?
(kahl eh oh seh-oo fee-MEH fah-voh-REE-tooh)

Can I get your opinion on something?
Posso ter a sua opinião sobre algo?
(POH-soh TEHR ah soo-ah oh-pee-nee-own soo-breh AHL-goh)

So, what brings you here tonight?
Então, o que te trouxe aqui hoje à noite?
(EN-taum, oh keh cheh TROH-shih ah-kee ah-JOH ah noy-tchee)

What kind of food do you like?
Que tipo de comida você gosta?
(keh TEE-poh jee koh-MEE-dah vo-SEH gos-tah)

I love your outfit, where did you get it?
Adorei a sua roupa, onde você comprou?
(ah-doh-REH ah soo-ah ROO-pah, OHN-deh vo-SEH kohm-PROH-oo)

What do you like to do for exercise?
O que você gosta de fazer para se exercitar?
(oh keh vo-SEH gos-tah jee fah-ZEHR pah-rah see ehk-sehr-see-TAHR)

Can I get you anything else to drink?
Posso te oferecer mais alguma coisa para beber?
(POH-soh chee oh-feh-reh-SER mah-ees ahl-GOO-mah KO-ee-sah pah-rah beh-BEHR)

This is going really well, don't you think?
Isso está indo muito bem, você não acha?
(EE-soh EH-stah EEN-doh MOO-ee-toh behm, vo-SEH naum AH-shah)

What do you think of this restaurant/bar/place?
O que você acha deste restaurante/bar/lugar?
(oh keh vo-SEH AH-shah DEHS-tee reh-stow-RAHN-teh/bahr/loo-GAHR)

So, what are your plans for the weekend?
Então, quais são seus planos para o fim de semana?
(EN-taum, kwais saum seh-oos PLAN-oos pah-rah oh feem deh seh-MAH-nah)

What kind of books do you like to read?
Que tipo de livros você gosta de ler?
(keh TEE-poh jee LEE-vroos vo-SEH gos-tah jee leh)

You're really easy to talk to.
É muito fácil conversar com você.
(eh MOO-ee-toh EH-zee-oo kohn-vehR-sahr kohm vo-SEH)

Have you been to any good concerts lately?
Você foi a algum bom show recentemente?
(vo-SEH foh-ee ah ahl-goom bohm show reh-SEN-teh-men-tee)

I really like spending time with you.
Eu gosto muito de passar tempo com você.
(EH-oo gos-toh MOO-ee-toh deh pah-SAHR TEHM-poo kohm vo-SEH)

What's the best trip you've ever taken?
Qual é a melhor viagem que você já fez?
(kahl eh ah meh-LOOR vee-AH-jeh keh vo-SEH jah fehz)

I had a great time tonight.
Eu me diverti muito esta noite.
(EH-oo meh jee-VEHR-tee MOO-ee-toh EH-stah noy-tchee)

What's your favorite type of music?
Qual é o seu tipo de música favorito?
(kahl eh oh seh-oo TEE-poh jee MOO-SEE-kah fah-voh-REE-toh)

I'd love to see you again.
Eu adoraria te ver novamente.
(EH-oo ah-doh-REE-ah cheh vehr neh-vah-MEHN-chee)

Would you like to split the bill?
Você quer dividir a conta?
(vo-SEH kehR dee-VEE-deer ah KOHN-tah?)

SHOPPING

Do you have this in a different size/color?
Você tem isso em um tamanho/cor diferente?
(VOH-say tehn EE-soo ehn oom tah-MAN-yoh/kohr dee-fee-REN-teh?)

How much is this?
Quanto custa isso?
(KWAN-too KOOS-tah EE-soo?)

Is there a sale going on right now?
Tem alguma promoção acontecendo agora?
(tehm ahl-GOO-mah proh-moh-SAHW ah-kohn-TEH-see-NOO ah-GOH-rah?)

Do you offer any discounts or promotions?
Vocês oferecem algum desconto ou promoção?
(VOH-says oh-feh-REH-sehm AHL-goom deh-SKON-toh oh proh-moh-SAHW?)

Can I try this on?
Posso experimentar isso?
(POH-soo eks-peh-ree-men-TAHR EE-soo?)

Where are the fitting rooms located?
Onde ficam os provadores?
(OHN-deh FEE-kahm ohs proh-vah-DOH-rehs?)

How does this look on me?
Como fica isso em mim?
(KO-moh FEE-kah EE-soo ehn meem?)

Can you suggest any accessories to go with this?
Você pode sugerir algum acessório para combinar com isso?
(VOH-say POH-deh soo-zheh-REER AHL-goom ah-SEHSS-oh-ree-oh pah-rah kohm-bee-NAHR kohm EE-soo?)

What is your return policy?
Qual é a sua política de devolução?
(KWAL EH ah SOO-ah po-lee-TEE-kah deh deh-voh-loo-SAHW?)

Do you have a gift receipt?
Vocês têm recibo de presente?
(VOH-says teh-ehm reh-SEE-boo deh preh-ZEHN-teh?)

Can I pay with a credit card?
Posso pagar com cartão de crédito?
(POH-soo pah-GAHR kohm kahr-TAHW deh KREH-dee-toh?)

Is there an ATM nearby?
Tem um caixa eletrônico perto daqui?
(tehm oom KAH-shah eh-leh-TROH-nee-koh PEHR-too dah-KEE?)

Can I have a receipt, please?
Posso ter um recibo, por favor?
(POH-soo TEHR oom reh-SEE-boo, pohr fah-VOHR?)

How much is the tax on this item?
Qual é o imposto sobre este item?
(KWAL EH oo eem-POHS-too SOH-breh EH-steh EE-tehm?)

Is there a shipping fee for online orders?
Tem taxa de envio para pedidos online?
(tehm TAH-k-sah deh EHN-vee-yoh pah-rah peh-DEE-doos ohn-LEEN-ee?)

How long does it take for the item to be shipped?
Quanto tempo leva para o item ser enviado?
(KWAN-too TEHM-poh LEH-vah pah-rah oo EE-tehm sehr ehn-vee-AH-doh?)

Can I track my order online?
Posso rastrear meu pedido online?
(POH-soo rah-streh-AHR meh-oo peh-DEE-doh ohn-LEEN-ee?)

Is there a way to expedite the shipping?
Tem como acelerar o envio?
(tehm KOH-moh ah-seh-leh-RAHR oo EHN-vee-yoh?)

Do you ship internationally?
Vocês enviam para o exterior?
(VOH-says EHN-vee-yahm pah-rah oh ehk-steh-REE-ohr?)

Can I return the item by mail?
Posso devolver o item pelo correio?
(POH-soo deh-vohl-VEHR oo EE-tehm PEH-loh koh-REH-yoo?)

Do I need to pay for return shipping?
Preciso pagar pelo envio de devolução?
*(preh-SEE-doh pah-GAHR PEH-loh EHN-vee-yoh deh
deh-voh-loo-SAHW?)*

Can I exchange the item for a different size/color?
Posso trocar o item por outro tamanho/cor?
(POH-soo TROH-kahr oo EE-tehm pohr OH-troh tah-MAN-yoh/kohr?)

Is there a restocking fee for returns?
Tem taxa de reposição para devoluções?
(tehm TAH-k-sah deh reh-poh-SEE-sawn pah-rah deh-voh-loo-SAHW?)

Can I use a coupon code on this purchase?
Posso usar um código de cupom nesta compra?
*(POH-soo oo-SAHR oom koh-DEE-go deh KOO-pohm NEHSS-tah
KOHM-prah?)*

How long will the sale last?
Quanto tempo durará a promoção?
(KWAN-too TEHM-poh doo-RAH-rah ah proh-moh-sawn?)

What material is this made of?
De que material é feito isso?
(deh keh ma-teh-REE-ahl eh FEH-toh EE-soo?)

Can I wash this in the washing machine?
Posso lavar isso na máquina de lavar?
(POH-soo lah-VAHR EE-soo nah MAH-kee-nah deh lah-VAHR?)

Do you have any other styles similar to this?
Vocês têm outros estilos similares a este?
(VOH-says teh-ehm OH-trohs esh-TEE-loos see-mee-LAH-rehs ah EH-steh?)

Can I place a special order for this item?
Posso fazer um pedido especial deste item?
(POH-soo FEH-zer oom peh-DEE-doh speh-see-AWL DEH-steh EE-tehm?)

DIRECTIONS

Insert each location in the blank, where applicable.

Excuse me, can you tell me how to get to _____?
Com licença, você pode me dizer como chegar a _____?
(kohm lee-SEHN-shee, voh-SEH poo-deh meh DEE-zer kohm CHEH-gar ah _____?)

Could you help me find my way to _____?
Você poderia me ajudar a encontrar o caminho para _____?
(voh-SEH poo-deh-REE-ah meh ah-zhoo-DAHR ah ehn-kohn-TRAR kah-MEE-nyoo pah-rah _____?)

Do you know how I can get to _____?
Você sabe como chegar a _____?
(voh-SEH SAH-bee kohmoh CHEH-gar ah _____?)

Which way is _____?
Por onde fica _____?
(por OHN-deh FEE-kah _____?)

Can you give me directions to _____?
Você pode me dar as direções para _____?
(voh-SEH poo-deh meh dahr ahs dee-reh-SOWNSS pah-rah _____?)

I'm lost. Can you tell me how to get to _____?
Estou perdido. Você pode me dizer como chegar a _____?
(eh-STOH per-DEE-doh. voh-SEH poo-deh meh DEE-zer kohm CHEH-gar ah _____?)

I'm trying to find _____, can you point me in the right direction?
Estou tentando encontrar _____, você pode me indicar a direção certa?
(eh-STOH tehn-TOO-doh ehn-kohn-TRAHR _____, voh-SEH poo-deh meh een-DEE-kahr ah dee-reh-SOWN SEHR-tah?)

Can you tell me how far _____ is from here?
Você pode me dizer a distância de _____ daqui?
(voh-SEH poo-deh meh DEE-zer ah dis-TAHN-see-ah deh _____
DAH-kee?)

Is it far from here to _____?
É longe daqui até _____?
(eh LOHN-jee DAH-kee ah-TEE _____?)

Could you tell me how to get to _____ on foot/by car/by bus?
Você poderia me dizer como chegar a _____ a pé/de carro/de ônibus?
(voh-SEH poo-deh-REE-ah meh DEE-zer kohmoh CHEH-gar ah _____ ah
PEH/deh KAH-roh/deh OH-nee-BOOS?)

Go straight ahead.
Siga em frente.
(SEE-gah ehm FREHN-ji)

Turn left/right at the next corner.
Vire à esquerda/direita na próxima esquina.
(VEE-reh ah ehs-KEHR-dah/dee-REH-tah nah PROH-ksy-mah
ehs-KEEN-ah)

Cross the street.
Atravesse a rua.
(ah-tra-VEH-see ah ROO-ah)

Walk for _____ minutes.
Ande por _____ minutos.
(AHN-deh por _____ mee-NOO-tos)

Go past the _____ on your left/right.
Passe pelo/a _____ à sua esquerda/direita.
(PAH-seh peh-loh/ah _____ ah soo-ah ehs-KEHR-dah/dee-REH-tah)

It's on your left/right.
Está à sua esquerda/direita.
(eh-STAH ah soo-ah ehs-KEHR-dah/dee-REH-tah)

It's straight ahead/on the corner.
É em frente/na esquina.
(eh ehm FREHN-ji/nah ehs-KEEN-ah)

It's just around the corner.
É logo ali na esquina.
(eh LOH-goo AH-lee nah ehs-KEEN-ah)

It's a few blocks from here.
Fica a algumas quadras daqui.
(FEE-kah ah ahl-GOO-mahs KWA-drahs DAH-kee)

Can you show me on the map?
Você pode me mostrar no mapa?
(voh-SEH poo-deh meh shoh-WAH noh MAH-pah?)

Do you have a map?
Você tem um mapa?
(voh-SEH tehn oon MAH-pah?)

Where can I find a map?
Onde posso encontrar um mapa?
(OHN-deh POH-soh ehn-kohn-TRAR oon MAH-pah?)

Is there a tourist information office near here?
Tem algum posto de informações turísticas perto daqui?
(tehn ah-GOO-moom POHS-too deh een-fohr-mah-SOWNS too-RISS-tee-kahs PEHR-too DAH-kee?)

How do I get to the nearest gas station?
Como eu chego ao posto de gasolina mais próximo?
(KOH-moh eh-oo CHEH-goh ah-oo POHS-too deh gah-zoh-LEE-nah mahs PROH-ksy-moh?)

Can you recommend a good restaurant nearby?
Você pode me recomendar um bom restaurante próximo?
(voh-SEH poo-deh meh reh-koh-mehn-DAHR oon BOHM reh-stow-RAHN-tcheh PROH-ksy-moh?)

Where is the closest ATM/bank?
Onde fica o caixa eletrônico/banco mais próximo?
(OHN-deh FEE-kah oh KAI-shah eh-leh-TROH-nee-koh/BAHNG-koh mahs PROH-ksy-moh?)

Do you know of any good shopping centers/malls around here?
Você conhece algum bom centro comercial/shopping por aqui?
(voh-SEH koh-NEH-seh ah-GOO-moom bohm SEN-troh koh-mehr-see-AWL/SHOP-ping por ah-KEE?)

Where can I find a taxi stand?
Onde posso encontrar um ponto de táxi?
(OHN-deh POH-soh ehn-kohn-TRAR oon POHN-toh deh TA-ksee?)

Is there a subway/metro station nearby?
Tem uma estação de metrô/subway perto daqui?
(tehm OO-mah ehs-tah-SOWN deh MEH-troh/SUB-way PEHR-too DAH-kee?)

Take the train/bus to _____.
Pegue o trem/ônibus para _____.
(PEH-gyoo oh TREHM/ohn-EE-boos PAH-rah _____.)

BUSINESS CONVERSATION

What is the purpose of this meeting?
Qual é o objetivo desta reunião?
(kwahl eh oo oh-beh-jeh-tivo DEHS-tah reh-oo-nee-ao?)

Can you give me an update on the progress?
Você pode me dar uma atualização sobre o progresso?
(voh-seh poh-deh meh dahr ooh-mah ah-too-ah-lee-zah-sawn soh-breh ooh proh-greh-so?)

How can we improve our sales?
Como podemos melhorar nossas vendas?
(koh-moh poh-deh-mohs meh-loh-rahr NOH-sahs VEN-dahs?)

What are our strengths and weaknesses?
Quais são nossos pontos fortes e fracos?
(kwah-ees sao NOH-soos POHN-tos FOR-tehs ee FRA-kohs?)

Can you explain the process?
Você pode explicar o processo?
(voh-seh poh-deh ehks-plee-kahr oh proh-SEHS-so?)

What is the timeline for this project?
Qual é o cronograma deste projeto?
(kwahl eh oo KROH-noh-grah-mah DES-teh proh-jeh-toh?)

What are the key performance indicators?
Quais são os indicadores-chave de desempenho?
(kwah-ees sao oos een-dee-kah-dohsh-KEH-veh deh deh-sehm-peh-nyoh?)

What is the budget for this initiative?
Qual é o orçamento para esta iniciativa?
(kwahl eh oo or-sah-men-toh PAH-rah ES-tah een-see-ah-TEE-vah?)

Can you provide a progress report?
Você pode fornecer um relatório de progresso?
(voh-seh poh-deh fohr-neh-ser oom reh-lah-toh-ree deh proh-greh-so?)

What are the deliverables for this project?
Quais são os entregáveis para este projeto?
(kwah-ees sao oos en-treh-gah-vee-ays PAH-rah eh-steh proh-jeh-toh?)

How can we streamline the process?
Como podemos otimizar o processo?
(koh-moh poh-deh-mohs oh-tee-mee-zahr o proh-SEHS-so?)

Can you provide more information?
Você pode fornecer mais informações?
(voh-seh poh-deh fohr-neh-ser mah-eez een-for-mah-see-owns?)

What is the target audience?
Qual é o público-alvo?
(kwahl eh oo POO-blee-koh-AHL-voh?)

How can we cut costs?
Como podemos reduzir custos?
(koh-moh poh-deh-mohs reh-doo-zeer KOOS-tos?)

What are the risks involved?
Quais são os riscos envolvidos?
(kwah-ees sao oos RISK-os en-vohl-VEE-dohs?)

Can we schedule a follow-up meeting?
Podemos agendar uma reunião de acompanhamento?
*(poh-deh-mohs ah-jen-dahr OO-mah reh-oo-nee-ao deh
ah-kohm-pan-yah-MEN-toh?)*

What are the project milestones?
Quais são as etapas do projeto?
(kwah-ees sao as eh-TAP-as doh proh-jeh-toh?)

How can we better allocate our resources?
Como podemos alocar melhor nossos recursos?
(koh-moh poh-deh-mohs ah-loh-kahr meh-lhohr NOH-sohs reh-SOOR-sehs?)

Can you give me an estimate of the timeline?
Você pode me dar uma estimativa do cronograma?
(voh-seh poh-deh meh dahr OO-mah ehs-tee-mah-TEE-vah doh KROH-noh-grah-mah?)

What is the target completion date?
Qual é a data de conclusão alvo?
(kwahl eh ah DAH-tah deh kohn-kloo-ZAWN AHL-voh?)

Can we assign someone to this task?
Podemos designar alguém para esta tarefa?
(poh-deh-mohs deh-zhee-nyahr ah-LGUEHM PAH-rah ES-tah tahr-EH-fah?)

What are the customer needs?
Quais são as necessidades do cliente?
(kwah-ees sao as ne-sess-ee-dah-dehs doh KLEE-en-teh?)

How can we increase productivity?
Como podemos aumentar a produtividade?
(koh-moh poh-deh-mohs ah-oo-men-tahr ah proh-doo-tiv-ee-dah-deh?)

Can you clarify the expectations?
Você pode esclarecer as expectativas?
(voh-seh poh-deh es-kla-reh-sehr as ehks-pehk-tah-TEE-vas?)

What are the market trends?
Quais são as tendências do mercado?
(kwah-ees sao as ten-den-see-as doh mer-KAH-doh?)

Can you revise the proposal?
Você pode rever a proposta?
(voh-seh poh-deh REH-vehr ah proh-pos-tah?)

What is the competition doing?

O que a concorrência está fazendo?

(oh keh ah kohn-koh-RREN-see-ah EHSTAH fah-ZEN-doh?)

How can we differentiate ourselves?

Como podemos nos diferenciar?

(koh-moh poh-deh-mohs nohs dee-feh-ren-see-AHR?)

Can we get an extension on the deadline?

Podemos obter uma extensão do prazo?

(poh-deh-mohs ohb-TEHR OO-mah eks-ten-SAWN doh PRAH-zoh?)

What is the projected timeline?

Qual é o cronograma projetado?

(kwahl eh ooh kroh-noh-grah-mah proh-jeh-tah-doh?)

STAYING AT A HOTEL

What time is check-in/check-out?
Que horas são o check-in/check-out?
(kay OH-rahss sao oh check-in/check-out?)

Is there a restaurant on-site?
Tem restaurante no hotel?
(tem rehs-tow-RAHN-tche noh oh-TELL?)

Is breakfast included in my room rate?
O café da manhã está incluído na minha diária?
(oh KAH-feh dah mah-NYAH ehss-TAH een-kloo-EE-doh nah MEE-nyah dee-AH-reeah?)

Is there a shuttle service to the airport/train station?
Tem serviço de transporte para o aeroporto/estação de trem?
(tem sair-VEE-soo deh trahn-spoahr-teh pah-rah oh ay-roh-POHR-toh/ehss-tah-SOW deh trehng?)

Is there a fitness center or gym available?
Tem academia ou ginásio disponível?
(tem ah-kah-DEH-meeah ooh jee-NAH-see-oh dee-speh-nee-VEHL?)

Can I get a late check-out?
Posso fazer check-out mais tarde?
(POH-soh fah-ZEHR check-out mah-iss TAR-deh?)

Do you offer room service?
Vocês oferecem serviço de quarto?
(voh-SESS oh-fee-REH-sehm sair-VEE-soo deh KWOR-toh?)

Is there a pool?
Tem piscina?
(tem pee-SEE-nah?)

Is there a concierge desk to help with recommendations for local attractions?
Tem um balcão de concierge para ajudar com recomendações de atrações locais?
(tem oom bahl-COW deh kohn-see-EHR-zhe pah-rah ah-zoo-DAHR kohm reh-koh-mehn-dah-SEE-ohns deh ah-TRAH-syownss LOH-kahys?)

Is there a laundry service available?
Tem serviço de lavanderia disponível?
(tem sair-VEE-soo deh lah-vahn-DEH-reeah dee-speh-nee-VEHL?)

Is there a safe in the room?
Tem cofre no quarto?
(tem KOH-freh noh KWOHR-toh?)

Can you recommend a good local restaurant?
Vocês podem recomendar um bom restaurante local?
(voh-SESS poh-dehm reh-koh-mehn-DAHR oom bohm rehs-tow-RAHN-tche LOH-kahl?)

Is there a mini-bar in the room?
Tem um frigobar no quarto?
(tem oom free-goh-BAR noh KWOHR-toh?)

How do I access the internet in my room?
Como faço para acessar a internet no meu quarto?
(KOH-moh FAH-soh pah-rah ah-kay-SAH a een-tehr-NEH noh mayoo KWOHR-toh?)

Are there any nearby attractions worth visiting?
Existem atrações próximas que valem a pena visitar?
(ehks-ee-STEHM ah-trah-SOWNS PROH-ksee-mahsh keh VAH-lehm ah PEH-nah vee-zhee-TAHHR?)

What is the Wi-Fi password?
Qual é a senha do Wi-Fi?
(kwahl eh ah SEH-nyah doo wee-fee?)

Can I have extra towels/blankets/pillows, etc.?
Posso ter toalhas/cobertores/travesseiros extras, etc.?
(POH-soh tehr toh-AH-lyahs/ko-behr-TOH-ress/trah-veh-SSEY-rohss EHKS-trahss, ehtch?)

What is the best way to get to the city center?
Qual é a melhor maneira de chegar ao centro da cidade?
(kwahl eh ah MEH-lor mah-NAY-rah deh cheh-GAHR oh SEN-troh dah SEE-dah-deh?)

Is there a view from the room?
Tem vista do quarto?
(tem VEE-stah doh KWOHR-toh?)

Can I pay with a credit card?
Posso pagar com cartão de crédito?
(POH-soh pah-GAHR kohm kahr-TAH-oh deh KREH-dee-toh?)

Is there a balcony/patio in the room?
Tem varanda/pátio no quarto?
(tem vah-RAN-dah/PAH-chee-oh noh KWOHR-toh?)

Do you have a map of the local area?
Vocês têm um mapa da área local?
(voh-SESS teh-ehm oom MAH-pah dah ah-REH-ah LOH-kahl?)

What is the cancellation policy?
Qual é a política de cancelamento?
(kwahl eh ah poh-LEE-see-ah deh kahn-seh-lah-MEHN-toh?)

Is there parking available?
Tem estacionamento disponível?
(tem es-tah-see-oh-nah-MEHN-toh dee-speh-nee-VEHL?)

Can I book a tour through the hotel?
Posso reservar um passeio pelo hotel?
(POH-soh reh-sehr-VAHR oom pah-SAY-oh peh-loh oh-TELL?)

Is there air conditioning in the room?
Tem ar-condicionado no quarto?
(tem ahr-kohn-dee-see-oh-NAH-doh noh KWOHR-toh?)

Can I have a wake-up call?
Posso receber uma ligação de despertar?
(POH-soh reh-seh-BEHR oom-ah lee-gah-SOW deh deh-spehr-TAHHR?)

What amenities are included in the room?
Quais são as comodidades incluídas no quarto?
(KWYS sah-oohn ahss koh-moh-deh-DAD-eez een-kloo-EE-dahss noh KWOHR-toh?)

Can I get a taxi to the airport/train station?
Posso pegar um táxi para o aeroporto/estação de trem?
(POH-soh peh-GAHR oom TAHK-see pah-rah oh ah-eh-roh-POHR-toh/eh-stah-SOW deh trehng?)

Can you recommend any local activities or events?
Você pode recomendar alguma atividade ou evento local?
(voh-SEH poh-deh reh-koh-mehn-DAHR ahlgoo-MAH ah-tee-vee-DAH-jee oh eh-vehn-toh LOH-kahl?)

WEATHER

What's the weather like today?
Qual é o clima hoje?
(kwahl eh oh KLEE-mah oh-JEE?)

Will it rain today?
Vai chover hoje?
(vai SHOH-ver oh-JEE?)

Is it hot outside?
Está quente lá fora?
(eh-STAH KEHN-teh lah FAW-rah?)

Is it cold outside?
Está frio lá fora?
(eh-STAH free-oh lah FAW-rah?)

What's the temperature?
Qual é a temperatura?
(kwahl eh ah tem-peh-rah-TOO-rah?)

Will it be sunny tomorrow?
Vai fazer sol amanhã?
(vai fah-ZEHR sohl ah-mahn-YAH?)

Is there a chance of thunderstorms?
Há chance de tempestades?
(ah CHAHN-suh deh tehm-peh-STAH-dehs?)

Is it going to snow?
Vai nevar?
(vai neh-VAHR?)

What's the forecast for tomorrow?
Qual é a previsão para amanhã?
(kwahl eh ah preh-vee-ZAH-oo pah-rah ah-mahn-YAH?)

Is it windy outside?
Está ventando lá fora?
(eh-STAH vehn-TAHN-doh lah FAW-rah?)

What's the humidity like?
Como está a umidade?
(KOH-moh eh-STAH ah ooh-mee-DAH-jee?)

Is it foggy outside?
Está com neblina lá fora?
(eh-STAH kohm neh-BLEE-nah lah FAW-rah?)

Will it be clear tonight?
Vai ficar limpo esta noite?
(vai fee-KAHR LEEmpoh EHS-tah noh-EE-teh?)

What's the chance of precipitation?
Qual é a chance de precipitação?
(kwahl eh ah CHAHN-suh deh preh-see-peh-tah-SOWNG?)

Is it going to be humid?
Vai estar úmido?
(vai eh-STAHR OO-mee-doh?)

How hot does it get here in the summer?
Como é o calor aqui no verão?
(KOH-moh eh oh kah-LOHR ah-KEE noh veh-RHOWN?)

How cold does it get here in the winter?
Como é o frio aqui no inverno?
(KOH-moh eh oh free-oh ah-KEE noh een-VEHR-no?)

What's the average temperature this time of year?
Qual é a temperatura média nesta época do ano?
(kwahl eh ah tem-peh-rah-TOO-rah MEH-dee-ah NEHS-tah eh-POH-kah doh ah-noo?)

Is there a hurricane coming?
Vem aí um furacão?
(vehm ah-EE oong foo-rah-KAH-oo?)

What's the UV index?
Qual é o índice UV?
(kwahl eh oh EEN-deh-see UV?)

Are there any weather warnings?
Há algum aviso meteorológico?
(ah ahl-goom ah-VEE-zoo meh-tee-oh-roh-LOH-jee-koo?)

Is it safe to travel in this weather?
É seguro viajar nessas condições climáticas?
(eh seh-GOO-roh vyah-ZHAHR NEHS-sahs kohn-dee-SOWNS klee-MAH-tee-kahs?)

Will the weather affect my flight?
O clima vai afetar meu voo?
(oh KLEE-mah vai ah-feh-TAHR meh-oo voh?)

Are there any areas affected by flooding?
Alguma área foi afetada por enchentes?
(ahl-GOO-mah ah-REH-ah foh-ee ah-feh-TAH-dah pohr ehn-CHEHN-tehs?)

What's the best time to visit for good weather?
Qual é a melhor época para visitar com bom clima?
(kwahl eh ah MEH-lor eh-POH-kah pah-rah vee-zee-TAHR kohm bohng KLEE-mah?)

Is it a good time to go to the beach?
É uma boa época para ir à praia?
(eh oong-ah BOH-ah eh-POH-kah pah-rah eer ah PRAH-ee-ah?)

What's the temperature of the water?
Qual é a temperatura da água?
(kwahl eh ah tem-peh-rah-TOO-rah dah AH-gwah?)

What should I wear in this weather?

O que devo vestir nessas condições climáticas?

*(oh keh DEH-voh veh-STEEHR NEHS-sahs kohn-dee-SOWNS
klee-MAH-tee-kahs?)*

**What's the weather like in [name of place] during [name of
month/season]?**

Como é o clima em [nome do lugar] durante [nome do mês/estação]?

*(KOH-moh eh oh KLEE-mah ehm [NOH-meh doh loo-GAHR]
doo-RAHN-teh [NOH-meh doh mehs/eh-stah-SOWNG]?)*

What's the forecast for the next few days?

Qual é a previsão para os próximos dias?

*(kwahl eh ah preh-vee-ZOWNG pah-rah ohs PROH-ksee-mohs
DEE-ahs?)*

AT THE GYM

What are the gym hours?
Em que horário a academia abre/fecha?
(ehm kih oh-RAH-ree-oo ah ah-ka-DEH-mee-ah AH-bree/FEH-shah?)

Do you have any classes today?
Há alguma aula hoje?
(ah ahl-GOO-mah OW-lah OH-jee?)

Can I get a tour of the gym?
Posso fazer um tour pela academia?
(POH-soh fah-ZEH-oo oong toor PEL-ah ah-ka-DEH-mee-ah?)

Where are the lockers located?
Onde ficam os armários?
(OHN-deh FEE-kahm ohs ahrr-MAH-ree-oos?)

How much does it cost to use the gym?
Quanto custa para usar a academia?
(KWAHN-too KOOSH-tah pah-rah oo-ZAH-ree ah ah-ka-DEH-mee-ah?)

Can I borrow a towel?
Posso pegar uma toalha emprestada?
(POH-soh peh-GAHR OO-mah toh-AH-lyah ehm-PREH-stah-dah?)

Where is the water fountain?
Onde fica o bebedouro?
(OHN-deh FEE-kah oh beh-beh-DOH-roo?)

Do you have any yoga mats?
Você tem algum tapete de yoga?
(VOH-say tehng ahl-GOONG tah-PEH-tee deh YOH-gah?)

Is there a sauna here?
Tem sauna aqui?
(tehng SOW-nah ah-KEE?)

How do I use this machine?
Como uso essa máquina?
(KOH-moh OO-soh ESS-ah MAH-kee-nah?)

Can you spot me?
Pode me ajudar a levantar peso?
(POH-deh meh ah-zoo-DAHR ah leh-vahn-TAHR PEH-soo?)

Where can I find the dumbbells?
Onde encontro os halteres?
(OHN-deh ehn-KOHN-troh ohs hahl-TEH-rehs?)

Is there a locker room here?
Tem vestiário aqui?
(tehng vehs-tee-AH-ree-oo ah-KEE?)

How much does a personal trainer cost?
Quanto custa um personal trainer?
(KWAHN-too KOOSH-tah oong pehr-soh-NAHL TREH-ner?)

Can I use the treadmill?
Posso usar a esteira?
(POH-soo oo-ZAHR ah ehs-TEH-ee-rah?)

Is there a weight limit on the machines?
Existe limite de peso nas máquinas?
(ehks-SEES-tee lee-MEE-teh deh PEH-so nahs MAH-kee-nahs?)

Can I pay with a credit card?
Posso pagar com cartão de crédito?
(POH-soo pah-GAHR kohm kahr-TAH-oo deh KREH-dee-toh?)

Where can I find the exercise balls?
Onde encontro as bolas de exercício?
(OHN-deh ehn-KOHN-troh ahs BOH-lahs deh ehk-sehr-SEE-see-oh?)

How many reps and sets should I do?
Quantas repetições e séries devo fazer?
(KWAN-tahs reh-peh-tee-SOWNS ee SEH-ree-ehs DEH-voh FAY-zer?)

Do you offer group classes?
Vocês oferecem aulas em grupo?
(VOH-says oh-feh-REH-sehm AH-lahs ehn GROO-poo?)

Can I bring a friend to the gym?
Posso trazer um amigo para a academia?
(POH-soo TRAY-zehr oong ah-MEE-goh pah-rah ah ah-ka-DEH-mee-ah?)

Is there a pool here?
Tem piscina aqui?
(tehng pee-SEE-nah ah-KEE?)

How do I adjust the seat on this machine?
Comoajusto o assento dessa máquina?
(KOH-moh ah-JOO-stoh oh ah-SEN-too DEH-sah MAH-kee-nah?)

Are there any fitness classes available today?
Existem aulas de ginástica disponíveis hoje?
(ehks-EE-stem OW-lahs deh jee-NAHS-tee-kah dee-spoh-NEE-vehys OH-jee?)

Can I get a protein shake here?
Posso tomar um shake de proteína aqui?
(POH-soo toh-MAHR oong SHAH-kee deh proh-teh-EE-na ah-KEE?)

How often should I come to the gym?
Com que frequência devo vir para a academia?
(kohm keh free-KEHN-see-ah DEH-voh veer pah-rah ah ah-ka-DEH-mee-ah?)

Is there a dress code for the gym?
Existe um código de vestimenta para a academia?
(ehks-SEE-steh oong koh-DEE-goh deh veh-stee-MEHN-tah pah-rah ah ah-ka-DEH-mee-ah?)

Can you recommend a workout routine for me?
Você pode me recomendar uma rotina de exercícios?
*(VOH-say POH-deh meh reh-koh-mehn-DAHR OO-mah roh-TEE-nah
deh ehk-sehr-SEE-see-ohs?)*

How long is the free trial period?
Quanto tempo dura o período de teste grátis?
*(KWAHN-too TEHM-poh DOO-rah oh peh-REE-oh-doh deh TEH-steh
GRAH-tis?)*

Is there a discount for long-term membership?
Tem desconto para membros de longo prazo?
*(tehng deh-SKAWN-toh pah-rah MEHM-brohs deh LOHN-goo
PRAH-zoh?)*

DOCTOR OR HOSPITAL VISIT

Can you please examine me?
Você pode me examinar, por favor?
(voh-SEH poh-deh meh eh-kzah-MEE-nahr, por fah-VOR?)

What tests do I need to undergo?
Quais testes preciso fazer?
(KWY tehs-TEHS PREH-see-zoh FAH-zer?)

Do you need me to fast before any tests?
Preciso fazer jejum antes de algum exame?
*(PREH-see-zoh FAH-zer jeh-JOOM ahn-TEHS deh AHL-goom
eh-KSAH-meh?)*

How long will it take to get the test results?
Quanto tempo leva para obter os resultados dos exames?
*(KWAN-toh TEHM-poh LEH-vah pah-rah ohb-TEHR ohs
reh-sool-TEE-doosh dohs eh-KSAH-mesh?)*

What is the diagnosis?
Qual é o diagnóstico?
(KWAL eh oh dee-ahg-NOHS-tee-koh?)

What is the cause of my symptoms?
Qual é a causa dos meus sintomas?
(KWAL eh ah KOW-zah dohs MEH-oosh sin-TOH-mahs?)

Is the condition serious?
A condição é grave?
(ah kon-dee-SOW eh GRAH-veh?)

What are my treatment options?
Quais são minhas opções de tratamento?
(KWY sah-oh MEE-nhas ohp-SOWNS deh trah-tah-MEN-too?)

Can you explain the benefits and risks of each treatment option?
Você pode explicar os benefícios e riscos de cada opção de tratamento?
(voh-SEH poh-deh ehks-plee-KAHR ohs beh-neh-FEE-see-oosh ee REES-koosh deh KAH-dah ohp-SOWM deh trah-tah-MEN-too?)

What are the side effects of the medications you are prescribing?
Quais são os efeitos colaterais dos medicamentos que está receitando?
(KWY sah-oh eh-FEH-toosh koh-lah-teh-RAYS dohs meh-dee-kah-MEN-toosh keh eh-stah reh-seh-ee-TAHN-doh?)

Do I need to follow any special instructions while taking the medication?
Preciso seguir alguma instrução especial durante o tratamento?
(PREH-see-zoh say-GEEHR ahl-GOO-mah een-stroo-SOWM speh-shee-AHL doo-RAN-teh oh trah-tah-MEN-too?)

Can I continue with my current medications?
Posso continuar com meus medicamentos atuais?
(POH-soh koh-tee-noo-AHR koh meh-oosh meh-dee-kah-MEN-toosh ah-TWAH-ees?)

Can I stop taking the medication once the symptoms subside?
Posso parar de tomar o medicamento assim que os sintomas desaparecerem?
(POH-soh pah-RAHR deh toh-MAR oh meh-dee-kah-MEN-too ah-SEEM keh ohs sin-TOH-mahs deh-sah-pah-re-cer-em?)

How often should I come for a follow-up appointment?
Com que frequência devo retornar para uma consulta de acompanhamento?
(kohm keh freh-KWEN-see-ah DEH-voh reh-tohr-NAHR pah-rah oo-mah kohn-SOOL-tah deh ah-kohm-pah-NHA-men-too?)

Is there anything I can do to manage my symptoms at home?
Há algo que posso fazer para controlar meus sintomas em casa?
(ah AHL-goh keh POH-soh FAH-zer pah-rah kohn-troh-LAR meh-oosh sin-TOH-mahs ehn KA-sah?)

What lifestyle changes do I need to make to improve my health?
Que mudanças no estilo de vida preciso fazer para melhorar minha saúde?
(keh moo-DAN-sahs noh es-TEE-loh deh VEE-dah PREH-see-zoh FAH-zer pah-rah meh-lho-RAR MEE-nha sah-OO-deh?)

Can you recommend any specialists if needed?
Você pode me indicar algum especialista, se necessário?
(voh-SEH poh-deh meh een-dee-KAHR AHL-goom es-peh-see-ah-LEES-tah, seh neh-sah-SAH-ree-oh?)

Can you write me a prescription for this medication?
Você pode me receitar este medicamento?
(voh-SEH poh-deh meh reh-seh-ee-TAHR EH-steh meh-dee-kah-MEN-too?)

What is the best way to manage pain?
Qual é a melhor maneira de controlar a dor?
(KWAL eh ah MELH-or mah-NEH-rah deh kohn-troh-LAR ah dohr?)

Can I take over-the-counter medications with this prescription?
Posso tomar medicamentos sem prescrição junto com este receituário?
(POH-soh toh-MAHR meh-dee-kah-MEN-toosh seh-oo preh-skree-SOWNG ZHOO-toh kohm EH-steh reh-seh-ee-TWAH-ree-oh?)

How long should I rest after the procedure?
Por quanto tempo devo descansar após o procedimento?
(por KWAN-toh TEHM-poh DEH-voh dehs-KAHN-sahr ah-PROHS oh PROH-seh-dee-MEN-too?)

Can you refer me to a physical therapist?
Você pode me encaminhar para um fisioterapeuta?
(voh-SEH poh-deh meh ehn-kah-MEE-nahr pah-rah oong fee-zee-oh-teh-rah-PEH-oo-tah?)

What exercises can I do to improve my condition?
Quais exercícios posso fazer para melhorar minha condição?
(KWY ee-zer-SEE-see-oosh POH-soh FAH-zer pah-rah meh-lho-RAR MEE-nha kon-dee-SOWN?)

Can you explain the surgical procedure to me?
Você pode me explicar o procedimento cirúrgico?
(voh-SEH poh-deh meh ehks-plee-KAHR oh proh-seh-DEE-men-too see-ROOJ-ee-koh?)

Are there any potential risks or complications associated with this treatment?
Existem riscos ou complicações associados a este tratamento?
(ehks-ees-TEHM REES-kohs oh kohm-plee-kah-SOWNS ah-SOH-see-ah-dohs ah EH-steh trah-tah-MEN-too?)

Can you provide me with more information about this condition?
Você pode me fornecer mais informações sobre esta condição?
(voh-SEH poh-deh meh fohr-neh-SER mahs een-fohr-mah-SOWNS ah-SOH-breh EH-stah kon-dee-SOWN?)

What can I expect during the recovery process?
O que posso esperar durante o processo de recuperação?
(oh keh POH-soh es-peh-RAHR doo-RAN-tee o proh-SEH-soh deh reh-koo-peh-rah-SOWN?)

Can you recommend any lifestyle changes to help manage my condition?
Você pode recomendar mudanças no estilo de vida para ajudar a controlar minha condição?
(voh-SEH poh-deh reh-koh-mehn-DAHR moo-DAHN-sahs noh es-TEE-loh deh VEE-dah pah-rah ah-zoo-DAR ah kohn-troh-LAR MEE-nha kon-dee-SOWN?)

Do I need any tests or procedures before starting treatment?
Eu preciso de exames ou procedimentos antes de começar o tratamento?
(yoo PREH-see-zoh deh eh-SAH-mes oh proh-seh-DEE-men-toosh ahn-tes deh koh-MEH-sahr o trah-tah-MEN-too?)

Can you recommend any resources or support groups for me and my family?

Você pode recomendar recursos ou grupos de apoio para mim e minha família?

(voh-SEH poh-deh reh-koh-mehn-DAHR reh-SOHRS-soosh oh GROO-poosh deh ah-POY-oh pah-rah meh ee MEE-nha fah-MEE-lee-ah?)

COMMON GREETINGS

Hello
Olá
(oh-LAH)

Hi
Oi
(oy)

Hey
Ei
(EY)

Good morning
Bom dia
(bohm DEE-ah)

Good afternoon
Boa tarde
(boh-ah TAR-deh)

Good evening
Boa noite
(boh-ah NOY-cheh)

Howdy
Como vai?
(KOH-moh VAI)

Greetings
Saudações
(saw-dah-SOW-ns)

Salutations
Cumprimentos
(koohm-pree-MEN-toos)

What's up
E aí?
(eh AI)

How's it going
Como está indo?
(KOH-moh ess-TAH een-DOO)

How are you doing
Como você está?
(KOH-moh voh-SEH ess-TAH)

Nice to meet you
Prazer em conhecê-lo
(prah-ZEHR ehn koh-neh-SEH-loo)

Pleasure to meet you
Prazer em conhecê-lo
(prah-ZEHR ehn koh-neh-SEH-loo)

It's good to see you
É bom te ver
(eh bohm teh vehr)

Long time no see
Quanto tempo!
(KWAN-toh TEM-po)

What's new
O que há de novo?
(oh KEH ah deh NO-vo)

What's happening
O que está acontecendo?
(oh keh ess-TAH ah-kawn-TEH-sehn-doo)

What's going on
O que está acontecendo?
(oh keh ess-TAH ah-kawn-TEH-sehn-doo)

Yo
E aí?
(eh AI)

Sup
E aí?
(eh AI)

Hola
Olá
(oh-LAH)

Bonjour
Bom dia
(bohm DEE-ah)

Ciao
Tchau
(CHOW)

Konnichiwa
Konnichiwa
(koh-nee-chee-WAH)

Shalom
Shalom
(shah-LOM)

Namaste
Namastê
(nah-mahs-TAY)

Salaam
Salaam
(sah-LAHM)

Hallo
Olá
(oh-LAH)

Guten tag
Bom dia
(bohm DEE-ah)

BANKING

I'd like to open a new account.
Eu gostaria de abrir uma nova conta.
(ayoo goh-stah-REE-ah deh ah-BREER ooh-mah NOH-vah COHN-tah)

Can you help me with my account?
Você pode me ajudar com minha conta?
(voh-SEH poh-deh meh ah-joo-DAR cohm MEE-nya COHN-tah?)

I need to deposit some money into my account.
Eu preciso depositar dinheiro na minha conta.
(ayoo prey-SEE-zoh deh-poh-zee-TAHR dee-NHEE-roh nah MEE-nya COHN-tah)

I'd like to withdraw some cash.
Eu gostaria de sacar algum dinheiro.
(ayoo goh-stah-REE-ah deh sah-KAHR ahl-goom dee-NHEE-roh)

Can you please give me some change?
Você pode me dar troco, por favor?
(voh-SEH poh-deh meh dahr TROH-koh, poor fah-VOHR?)

What is the current interest rate on this account?
Qual é a taxa de juros atual nesta conta?
(kwahl eh ah TA-kah deh JOO-rohss ahk-TOO-ahl NESS-tah COHN-tah?)

How can I check my account balance?
Como posso verificar o saldo da minha conta?
(KO-moh POH-soh veh-ree-fee-KAHR oh SAHL-doh dah MEE-nya COHN-tah?)

Can you explain these fees to me?
Você pode me explicar essas taxas?
(voh-SEH poh-deh meh ehks-plee-KAHR EH-sahss TA-kahss?)

What types of accounts do you offer?
Que tipos de contas você oferece?
(keh TEE-pos deh KOHN-tahs voh-SEH oh-fah-REH-see?)

I'd like to apply for a loan.
Eu gostaria de solicitar um empréstimo.
*(ayoo goh-stah-REE-ah deh soh-lee-see-TAHR oom
ehm-PREH-stee-moh)*

What documents do I need to open an account?
Quais documentos preciso para abrir uma conta?
*(kwahys doh-koo-MEN-toos prey-SEE-zoh pah-rah ah-BREER ooh-mah
COHN-tah?)*

Can you help me activate my debit card?
Você pode me ajudar a ativar meu cartão de débito?
*(voh-SEH poh-deh meh ah-joo-DAR ah ah-tee-VAHR meh-oo
kahr-TAHW deh DEH-bee-toh?)*

What is the daily withdrawal limit?
Qual é o limite diário de saque?
(kwahl eh oh LEE-mee-teh DEE-ah-ree-oh deh SAH-keh?)

Can you assist me with online banking?
Você pode me ajudar com o banco online?
(voh-SEH poh-deh meh ah-joo-DAR kohm bohn-koh ohn-LINE?)

Can I get a receipt for my transaction?
Posso obter um recibo para a minha transação?
*(POH-soh ohb-TEHR oom reh-SEE-boo pah-rah a MEE-nya
trahn-sah-KAHW?)*

What is the routing number for this bank?
Qual é o número de roteamento deste banco?
*(kwahl eh oh NOO-meh-roh deh roh-teh-AH-mehn-too DEHS-teh
BAHN-koh?)*

How long will it take to process my transaction?
Quanto tempo levará para processar minha transação?
(KWAN-toh TEHM-poh leh-vah-RAH pah-rah proh-SEH-sahr MEE-nya trahn-sah-KAHW?)

Can I set up automatic payments?
Posso configurar pagamentos automáticos?
(POH-soh kohng-fee-goo-RAHR pah-gah-MEN-toos oh-toh-MAH-tee-kohs?)

What is the minimum balance requirement for this account?
Qual é o requisito de saldo mínimo para esta conta?
(kwahl eh oh REH-kwee-ZEE-toh deh SAHL-doh mee-NEE-moh pah-rah EHSS-tah COHN-tah?)

Can you explain the overdraft protection options?
Você pode explicar as opções de proteção contra saldo negativo?
(voh-SEH poh-deh ehks-plee-KAHR ahs ohp-SOH-ess deh proh-teh-KAHW KON-trah SAHL-doh neh-gah-TEE-voh?)

Can you help me order new checks?
Você pode me ajudar a pedir novos cheques?
(voh-SEH poh-deh meh ah-joo-DAR ah peh-DEER NOH-voos CHEH-kees?)

Can you explain the rewards program?
Você pode explicar o programa de recompensas?
(voh-SEH poh-deh ehks-plee-KAHR oh proh-GRAH-mah deh reh-KOHM-pehn-sahs?)

Can I get a cashier's check?
Posso obter um cheque administrativo?
(POH-soh ohb-TEHR oom CHEH-keh ahdmee-nees-trah-TEE-voh?)

Can you provide me with a bank statement?
Você pode me fornecer um extrato bancário?
(voh-SEH poh-deh meh fohr-neh-SEHR oom ehk-TRAH-toh bahn-KAH-ree-oh?)

Can I make a transfer to another bank?
Posso fazer uma transferência para outro banco?
(POH-soh fah-ZEHR ooh-mah trahnss-feh-REHN-see-ah pah-rah
OH-troh BAHN-koh?)

Can I get a notarized document here?
Posso obter um documento notarizado aqui?
(POH-soh ohb-TEHR oom doh-koo-MEN-toh noh-tah-ree-ZAH-doh
ah-KEE?)

Can you help me with a foreign currency exchange?
Você pode me ajudar com uma troca de moeda estrangeira?
(voh-SEH poh-deh meh ah-joo-DAR kohm OO-mah TROH-kah deh
MOH-eh-dah es-trahn-JEH-rah?)

Can I open a joint account with my spouse/partner?
Posso abrir uma conta conjunta com meu cônjuge / parceiro?
(POH-soh ah-BREER OO-mah COHN-tah kohn-ZHOON-tah kohm
MEH-oo KOHN-zhoo-JE / pahr-SEH-roo?)

What is the interest rate for this savings account?
Qual é a taxa de juros para esta conta poupança?
(kwahl eh ah TAH-kah deh ZHOH-roos pah-rah EHSS-tah COHN-tah
poh-PAHN-sah?)

COMMON TRAVELER QUESTIONS

What are the visa requirements for visiting this country?
Quais são os requisitos de visto para visitar este país?
(KWAY-sow soo re-kee-ZHEE-toosh dee VEE-soo pah-rah vee-zhee-TAR esh-TEE pah-EEsh?)

What is the local emergency phone number?
Qual é o número de telefone de emergência local?
(KWAHL eh oo NOO-meh-roo deh teh-leh-FOH-neh deh eh-mehr-ZHEN-syah LOH-kahl?)

Can I use my credit card here? -
Posso usar meu cartão de crédito aqui?
(POH-soh oo-ZAR may-oo kahr-TAH-ooh deh KREH-dee-too ah-KEE?)

What is the public transportation system like?
Como é o sistema de transporte público?
(KOH-moo eh oo sis-TEH-mah deh trahn-SPOR-tay POO-blee-koo?)

How do I navigate the local transportation system?
Como navego no sistema de transporte local?
(KOH-moo nah-VEH-goh noh sis-TEH-mah deh trahn-SPOR-tay LOH-kahl?)

What are the local laws and regulations?
Quais são as leis e regulamentos locais?
(KWAY-sow sah-ooh ays ee reh-goo-lah-MEN-toosh LOH-kah-oosh?)

Where can I find a pharmacy?
Onde posso encontrar uma farmácia?
(OHN-deh POH-soh en-kohn-TRAHR oo-mah fahr-MAH-syah?)

What is the local dress code?
Qual é o código de vestimenta local?
(KWAHL eh oo KOH-dee-goh deh veys-tee-MEN-tah LOH-kahl?)

Are there any areas I should avoid for safety reasons?
Existem áreas que devo evitar por razões de segurança?
(eh-shis-TEHM AH-ree-ahs keh DEH-voh e-vee-TAHR por rah-ZHOWNS deh seh-goo-RAHN-sah?)

What is the local time zone?
Qual é o fuso horário local?
(KWAHL eh oo FOH-soo oh-RAR-ee-oo LOH-kahl?)

How do I convert between currencies?
Como faço para converter entre moedas?
(KOH-moo FAH-soh pah-rah kohn-VEHR-tehr EN-treh mwed-as?)

Where can I find public restrooms?
Onde posso encontrar banheiros públicos?
(OHN-deh POH-soh en-kohn-TRAHR bahn-YEH-roosh POO-blee-kohs?)

What are the local customs and traditions?
Quais são os costumes e tradições locais?
(KWAY-sow sah-ooh oos koh-STOO-mesh ee trah-dee-SHOWNS LOH-kah-oosh?)

How do I get to the airport/train station/bus station?
Como chego ao aeroporto/estação de trem/rodoviária?
(KOH-moh CHEH-goh ah-oh eh-roh-POHR-toh/eh-stah-SOW deh TREH-ooh/roh-doh-vee-AH-ree-ah?)

Can you recommend any good restaurants around here?
Você pode recomendar algum bom restaurante por aqui?
(voh-SEH poh-deh reh-koh-men-DAHR ahl-gohm boh-ooh res-tow-RAN-tay por ah-KEE?)

What are some popular tourist attractions in this area?
Quais são as atrações turísticas populares nesta área?
(KWAY-sow sah-ooh ahs ah-TRAH-sow-esh too-ris-TEE-kahs po-poo-LAH-res NES-tah ah-REE-ah?)

How much does this cost?
Quanto custa isso?
(KWAN-toh KOOSH-tah EE-soo?)

Where is the nearest ATM?
Onde fica o caixa eletrônico mais próximo?
(OHN-deh FEE-kah oo KAH-ee-shah eh-leh-TROH-nee-koh mahsh proh-KSEE-moh?)

What are some phrases I should know in the local language?
Quais são algumas frases que devo saber no idioma local?
(KWAY-sow sah-ooh ahl-GOO-mas FRAH-zesh keh DEH-voh sah-BEHR noo ee-jyoh-MAH LOH-kahl?)

Can I drink the tap water here?
Posso beber água da torneira aqui?
(POH-soh beh-BEHR AH-gwah dah toh-REH-rah ah-KEE?)

How do I say "please" and "thank you" in the local language?
Como digo "por favor" e "obrigado" no idioma local?
(KOH-moh DEE-goh "por fah-VOHR" ee "oh-bree-GAH-doh" noo ee-jyoh-MAH LOH-kahl?)

What is the exchange rate for my currency?
Qual é a taxa de câmbio para a minha moeda?
(KWAHL eh ah TA-k-sah deh KAHM-byoh pah-rah ah MAH-nyah mwed-ah?)

Where can I buy a SIM card for my phone?
Onde posso comprar um cartão SIM para o meu telefone?
(OHN-deh POH-soh kohm-prahr oom kahr-TAH-ooh SEEM pah-rah oo may-oo teh-leh-FOH-neh?)

How do I ask for directions?
Como pedir direções?
(KOH-moh peh-DEER dee-reh-SHOWNS?)

Is there a local tourist office where I can get more information?
Existe um escritório de turismo local onde posso obter mais informações?
(eh-SHEES-teh oong es-kree-STOH-ree deh too-REEZ-moh LOH-kahl OHN-deh POH-soh ohb-TEHR mahs een-fohr-mah-SHOWNS?)

Can you recommend any local festivals or events?
Você pode recomendar alguns festivais ou eventos locais?
(voh-SEH poh-deh reh-koh-men-DAHR ahl-GOONS fes-tee-VAH-ee-ooh oh e-vehn-TOOS LOH-kahys?)

What is the best way to get around the city?
Qual é a melhor maneira de se locomover na cidade?
(KWAHL eh ah MEH-lor mah-NEH-rah deh seh loh-koh-MOH-ver nah SEE-dah-deh?)

What is the local currency?
Qual é a moeda local?
(KWAHL eh ah MOY-dah LOH-kahl?)

How do I call a taxi?
Como chamar um táxi?
(KOH-moh sha-MAHR oong TAHK-see?)

Is there a dress code for this place?
Existe um código de vestimenta para este lugar?
(eh-SHEES-teh oong KOH-dee-goh deh vehs-tee-MEN-tah pah-rah EH-steh loo-GAHR?)

COMMON RESPONSES TO QUESTIONS

Yes, that's correct.
Sim, está correto.
(seem, ehs-tah koh-REH-toh)

No, that's not accurate.
Não, isso não está preciso.
(não, EE-soh não ehs-TAH preh-SEE-soh)

I'm not sure, let me check and get back to you.
Não tenho certeza, deixe-me verificar e retornar para você.
(não TEH-nyoh sehr-TEH-zah, DAY-sheh-meh veh-ree-fee-KAHR eh reh-tohr-NAHR pah-rah voh-SAY)

Can you please repeat the question?
Você pode repetir a pergunta, por favor?
(voh-SEH poh-deh reh-peh-TEER ah PEHRN-tah, pohr fah-VOHR?)

Sorry, I didn't understand your question.
Desculpe, não entendi a sua pergunta.
(dehs-KOOL-peh, não ehn-TEN-dee ah SOO-ah PEHRN-tah)

To be honest, I don't have an answer for that.
Para ser honesto, eu não tenho uma resposta para isso.
(PAH-rah sehr oh-NES-too, eh-oo não TEH-nyoh OO-mah reh-SPOHS-tah pah-rah EE-soh)

It depends on the context.
Isso depende do contexto.
(EE-soh deh-PEHN-deh doh kohn-TEX-toh)

That's a great question, let me think about it for a moment.
Essa é uma ótima pergunta, deixe-me pensar um pouco sobre isso.
(EH-sah eh OO-mah OH-tee-mah PEHRN-tah, DAY-sheh-meh pehn-SAHR oohm POH-koh soh-BREH EE-soh)

I'm afraid I don't know.
Receio que não sei.
(reh-SEY-oh keh não say)

That's a good point, let me think about it.
Isso é um bom ponto, deixe-me pensar sobre isso.
(EE-soh eh oohm BOHM POHN-toh, DAY-sheh-meh pehn-SAHR soh-BREH EE-soh)

Absolutely.
Absolutamente.
(ahb-soh-loo-TA-men-tee)

Definitely not.
Definitivamente não.
(deh-fee-nee-tee-VA-men-tee não)

Possibly.
Possivelmente.
(poh-SEE-vehl-men-tee)

That's a tough one.
Essa é difícil.
(EH-sah eh dee-fee-SEEL)

I can see both sides of the argument.
Eu consigo ver ambos os lados da discussão.
(eh-oo kohn-SEE-goh vehr AHM-bohs ohs LAH-dohs dah doo-see-SOWH)

It's hard to say for sure.
É difícil dizer com certeza.
(eh dee-fee-SEEL dee-ZEHR kohm sehr-TEH-zah)

I'm inclined to agree/disagree with you.
Eu estou inclinado a concordar/discordar com você.
(eh-oo ehs-TOH-oo een-k-lEE-nah-doh ah kohn-kohr-DAHR/dee-skohn-kohr-DAHR kohm voh-SEH)

I think so, but I'm not entirely certain.
Eu acho que sim, mas não tenho certeza absoluta.
*(eh-oo AH-shoh keh seem, mahs não TEH-nyoh sehr-teh-za
ahb-soh-loo-tah)*

Not necessarily.
Não necessariamente.
(não neh-sess-ah-REE-ah-men-tee)

That's a valid point.
Esse é um ponto válido.
(EH-seh eh oohm POHN-toh VAH-lee-doh)

I see what you're saying.
Entendi o que você está dizendo.
(ehn-TEN-dee oh keh voh-SEH ehss-TAH dee-ZEHN-doh)

That's an interesting perspective.
Essa é uma perspectiva interessante.
(EH-sah eh OO-mah per-spehk-TEE-vah in-teh-REHSS-tahn-teh)

That's a possibility.
Essa é uma possibilidade.
(EH-sah eh OO-mah poh-see-bee-lee-DAH-deh)

I'm open to discussion.
Estou aberto*(a)* a discussão.
(ehs-TOH ab-ehr-toh ah doo-see-SOWH)

I'm not convinced.
Não estou convencido*(a)*.
(não ehs-TOH kohn-vehn-SEE-doh)

That's a tricky question.
Essa é uma pergunta complicada.
(EH-sah eh OO-mah PEHRN-tah kohm-plee-KAH-dah)

Let me clarify what I mean.
Deixe-me esclarecer o que eu quero dizer.
(DEY-shah-meh ehs-kla-REH-sehr ooh keh eh-oo KEH-roh dee-ZEHR)

I agree with you to a certain extent.
Concordo com você em certa medida.
(kohn-kohr-DOO kohm voh-SEH ehn sehr-tah meh-DEE-dah)

That's a fair question.
Essa é uma pergunta justa.
(EH-sah eh OO-mah PEHRN-tah JOOS-tah)

Let me think about it and get back to you.
Deixe-me pensar sobre isso e voltarei para você.
(DAY-sheh-meh pehn-SAHR soh-BREH EE-soh eh vol-tah-RAY pah-rah voh-SAY)

PETS

Dog
Cão
(KOW)

Cat
Gato
(GAH-toh)

Bird
Pássaro
(PAH-sah-roh)

Fish
Peixe
(PAY-shuh)

Hamster
Hamster
(ahm-STAIR)

Guinea pig
Porquinho-da-índia
(por-KEEN-yoo dah EEN-dee-ah)

Rabbit
Coelho
(ko-EH-lyoo)

Ferret
Furão
(foo-RAY-oh)

Hedgehog
Ouriço
(oh-REE-soh)

Chinchilla
Chinchila
(sheen-CHEE-lah)

Mouse
Rato
(RAH-toh)

Rat
Rato
(RAH-toh)

Gerbil
Gerbo
(JAYR-boh)

Snake
Cobra
(KOH-brah)

Lizard
Lagarto
(lah-GAHR-toh)

Turtle
Tartaruga
(tar-tah-ROO-gah)

Tortoise
Tartaruga
(tar-tah-ROO-gah)

Hermit crab
Caranguejo eremita
(kah-rahn-GAY-jo eh-ray-MEE-tah)

Tarantula
Tarântula
(tah-RAHN-too-lah)

Scorpion
Escorpião
(ess-kor-pee-AWN)

Bearded dragon
Dragão barbudo
(drah-GOWN bar-BOO-doh)

Sugar glider
Planador açucarado
(plah-na-DOR ah-soo-kah-RAH-doh)

Prairie dog
Cão da pradaria
(KOW da prah-DAH-ree-ah)

Skunk
Gambá
(gam-BAH)

Pot-bellied pig
Porco de barriga
(POR-koo jee bah-HEE-gah)

Miniature horse
Cavalo miniatura
(kah-VAH-loh mee-nee-ah-TOO-rah)

Goat
Cabra
(KAH-brah)

Sheep
Ovelha
(oh-VEH-lyah)

Chicken
Galinha
(gah-LEE-nyah)

Duck
Pato
(PAH-toh)

COLORS

Red
Vermelho
(vair-meh-lyoo)

Blue
Azul
(ah-zool)

Green
Verde
(VEHR-deh)

Yellow
Amarelo
(ah-mah-REH-loo)

Orange
Laranja
(lah-RAHN-jah)

Purple
Roxo
(HOH-shoo)

Pink
Rosa
(HO-sah)

Brown
Marrom
(mah-HOHM)

Black
Preto
(PREH-too)

White
Branco
(BRAHN-koo)

Gray
Cinza
(SEEN-zah)

Navy
Marinho
(mah-REEN-yoo)

Turquoise
Turquesa
(toor-KEH-zah)

Magenta
Magenta
(mah-JEN-tah)

Maroon
Borgonha
(bor-GO-nyah)

Olive
Oliva
(oh-LEE-vah)

Teal
Azul-petróleo
(ah-ZOOL peh-troh-LEH-oo)

Lavender
Lavanda
(lah-VAHN-dah)

Beige
Bege
(BEH-jee)

Cyan
Ciano
(SEE-ah-noh)

Salmon
Salmão
(sal-MOWN)

Gold
Dourado
(doh-RAH-doh)

Silver
Prateado
(prah-TEH-ah-doh)

Indigo
Índigo
(EEN-dee-goh)

Fuchsia
Fúcsia
(FOOK-see-ah)

Charcoal
Carvão
(kar-VOW)

Peach
Pêssego
(PEH-sseh-goh)

Mint
Mentolado
(mehn-toh-LAH-doh)

Tan
Bronzeado
(bron-zeh-AH-doh)

Ivory
Marfim
(MAHR-feem)

Burgundy
Borgonha
(bor-GO-nyah)

Mustard
Mostarda
(moh-STAH-dah)

Rust
Ferrugem
(feh-ROO-jehm)

Teal
Azul-petróleo
(ah-ZOOL peh-troh-LEH-oo)

Coral
Coral
(koh-RAHL)

Lavender
Lavanda
(lah-VAHN-dah)

Olive
Oliva
(oh-LEE-vah)

Sienna
Siena
(see-EN-ah)

Sky blue
Azul-celeste
(ah-ZOOL seh-LEH-steh)

Lilac
Lilás
(lee-LAHS)

Plum
Ameixa
(ah-MEH-shah)

Aqua
Água
(AH-gwah)

Khaki
Cáqui
(KAH-kee)

Slate
Ardósia
(ahr-DOH-zee-ah)

Apricot
Damasco
(dah-MAHS-koo)

Emerald
Esmeralda
(ehs-meh-RAHL-dah)

Navy blue
Azul-marinho
(ah-ZOOL mah-REEN-yoo)

Pewter
Estanho
(eh-STAH-nyoo)

Brick red
Vermelho-tijolo
(vair-mehl-yoo tee-JOH-loo)

Cream
Creme
(KREH-meh)

Chocolate
Chocolate
(shoh-koh-LAHT)

Turmeric
Açafrão
(ah-SAF-raohn)

Mauve
Malva
(MAHL-vah)

Salmon
Salmão
(sal-MOWN)

Bronze
Bronze
(BRAWN-zee)

Peacock blue
Azul-pavão
(ah-ZOOL pah-VAHN)

Khaki green
Verde-cáqui
(VEHR-deh KAH-kee)

Tangerine
Tangerina
(tahn-jeh-REE-nah)

Coral pink
Rosa-coral
(HO-sah koh-RAHL)

Olive green
Verde-oliva
(VEHR-deh oh-LEE-vah)

NUMBERS

One
Um
(oo[m])

Two
Dois
(DOYSH)

Three
Três
(TREHSH)

Four
Quatro
(KWUH-troo)

Five
Cinco
(SING-koo)

Six
Seis
(SAYSH)

Seven
Sete
(SEH-tay)

Eight
Oito
(OY-too)

Nine
Nove
(NO-vay)

Ten
Dez
(DEHSH)

Eleven
Onze
(OHN-zay)

Twelve
Doze
(DOH-zay)

Thirteen
Treze
(TREH-zay)

Fourteen
Catorze
(kah-TOHR-zay)

Fifteen
Quinze
(KEENG-zay)

Sixteen
Dezesseis
(deh-zeh-SAYSH)

Seventeen
Dezessete
(deh-zeh-SEH-tay)

Eighteen
Dezoito
(deh-ZOY-too)

Nineteen
Dezenove
(deh-zay-NO-vay)

Twenty
Vinte
(VEEN-tay)

HANDLING A RUDE PERSON

I'm sorry, but I won't tolerate that kind of behavior.
Eu sinto muito, mas eu não vou tolerar esse tipo de comportamento.
(ehu SEEN-too MOO-TOO, mahs ehu nown VOW toh-LEH-rahr EH-see TEE-poh dee kohm-pohr-tah-MEN-too)

I don't appreciate the way you're speaking to me.
Eu não aprecio a maneira como você está falando comigo.
(ehu nown ah-PREH-see-oh ah mah-NAY-rah KOH-moo voh-SEH eh-stah fah-LAHN-doo kohm MEE-goo)

I understand you're upset, but please don't take it out on me.
Eu entendo que você está chateado, mas por favor, não descarregue isso em mim.
(ehu ehn-TEN-doo keh voh-SEH eh-stah shah-teh-AH-doo, mahs poor fah-VOHR, nown deh-skahr-GOO-eh EE-soh ehn meem)

Let's try to stay calm and talk this through.
Vamos tentar ficar calmos e conversar sobre isso.
(VAH-moos TEHN-tahr FEE-kahr KAL-moosh ee kohn-vehr-SAR SOH-bree EE-soo)

Can we please have a civil conversation?
Podemos por favor ter uma conversa civilizada?
(POH-deh-moosh poor fah-VOHR TEHR OO-mah kohn-vehr-SAH see-vee-lee-ZAH-dah)

Please watch your language when you're talking to me.
Por favor, cuidado com a linguagem quando você estiver falando comigo.
(pohr fah-VOHR, kwih-DAH-doo kohm a leeng-GWAH-jeng KWAN-doo voh-SEH eh-stee-vair fah-LAHN-doo kohm-EE-goo)

I don't deserve to be spoken to in that way.
Eu não mereço ser falado dessa maneira.
(ehu nown meh-REH-soh sehr fah-LAH-doo DEH-sah mah-NAY-rah)

Your behavior is unacceptable.
Seu comportamento é inaceitável.
(seh-oo kohm-pohr-tah-MEN-too eh ee-nah-seh-ee-TAH-vehl)

I'm not going to engage in this kind of disrespect.
Eu não vou me envolver em falta de respeito desse tipo.
(ehu nown vow meh ehn-vohl-VEHR ehm FAHL-tah deh res-peh-TOH DEHS-see TEE-poh)

I won't be spoken to like that.
Eu não vou ser falado assim.
(ehu nown vow sehr fah-LAH-doo ah-SEEM)

I won't tolerate rude or aggressive behavior.
Eu não vou tolerar comportamentos rudes ou agressivos.
(ehu nown vow toh-LEH-rahr kohm-pohr-tah-MEN-toosh ROO-dess oh ah-greh-SEE-vohsh)

Please treat me with respect.
Por favor, trate-me com respeito.
(pohr fah-VOHR, TRAH-teh-meh kohm res-peh-TOO)

I don't think it's appropriate to speak to anyone in that manner.
Eu não acho apropriado falar com alguém dessa maneira.
(ehu nown AH-shoo ah-proh-PREE-ah-doo fah-LAHR kohm ah-LGEHM DEH-sah mah-NAY-rah)

I won't engage in an argument with you.
Eu não vou entrar em uma discussão com você.
(ehu nown vow en-TRAHR ehm OO-mah doo-see-SOWNG kohm voh-SEH)

I'd appreciate it if you would speak to me more respectfully.
Eu agradeceria se você falasse comigo com mais respeito.
(ehu ah-grah-deh-SEE-ree-ah seh voh-SEH fah-LAH-see kohm-EE-goo kohm mahs res-peh-TOO)

Please lower your voice.
Por favor, abaixe sua voz.
(pohr fah-VOHR, ah-BOW-jee soo-ah VOHZ)

Your behavior is making me uncomfortable.
Seu comportamento está me deixando desconfortável.
(seh-oo kohm-pohr-tah-MEN-too EH-stah meh day-SHAHN-doo deh-skohm-FOHR-tah-vehl)

I won't put up with this kind of treatment.
Eu não vou tolerar esse tipo de tratamento.
(ehu nown vow toh-LEH-rahr EH-see TEE-poh deh trah-tah-MEN-too)

Please show some respect.
Por favor, mostre um pouco de respeito.
(pohr fah-VOHR, MOH-streh oom POH-koo deh res-peh-TOO)

I won't stand for this.
Eu não vou aceitar isso.
(ehu nown vow ah-seh-ee-TAHR EE-soh)

Please stop speaking to me in that manner.
Por favor, pare de falar comigo dessa maneira.
(pohr fah-VOHR, PAH-reh jee fah-LAH koh-MEE-goo DEHS-sah mah-NAY-rah)

I'm not going to listen to this kind of language.
Eu não vou escutar esse tipo de linguagem.
(ehu nown vow es-koo-TAHR EH-see TEE-poh deh leen-gwah-JENG)

I won't tolerate this disrespectful behavior.
Eu não vou tolerar esse comportamento desrespeitoso.
(ehu nown vow toh-LEH-rahr EH-see kohm-pohr-tah-MEN-too desh-reh-speh-ee-TOH-soo)

Please calm down and let's talk rationally.
Por favor, acalme-se e vamos conversar racionalmente.
(pohr fah-VOHR, ah-kahl-meh-seh e VAH-moos kohn-vehhr-SAR rah-see-oh-nahl-MEN-teh)

I don't appreciate being spoken to like that.
Eu não aprecio ser falado assim.
(ehu nown ah-PREH-see-oh sehr fah-LAH-doo ah-SEEM)

Please refrain from using offensive language.
Por favor, evite usar linguagem ofensiva.
*(pohr fah-VOHR, eh-VEE-teh oo-SAR lee-NGWAH-jeng
oh-fehn-SEE-vah.)*

Your behavior is unacceptable.
Seu comportamento é inaceitável.
(seh-oo kohm-pohr-tah-MEN-too EH een-ah-SEH-ee-TAH-vehl)

Please treat me with respect.
Por favor, trate-me com respeito.
(pohr fah-VOHR, TRAH-teh-meh kohm res-peh-TOO)

Your language is offensive.
Sua linguagem é ofensiva.
(SOO-ah leen-GWAH-zhem EH oh-fen-SEE-vah)

I won't tolerate any further rudeness.
Não vou tolerar mais grosserias.
(não vow toh-LEH-rahr mah-ees groh-seh-REE-ahs)

GOING TO A PHYSICIAN

Hello, I'm here for my appointment.
Olá, estou aqui para minha consulta.
(oh-LAH, es-TOH ah-KEE pah-rah MEE-nya kon-SUL-ta.)

I've been experiencing some health problems lately.
Tenho tido alguns problemas de saúde ultimamente.
(TEN-yoh TEE-doh AL-guns pro-BLE-mas di SAU-de ul-ti-ma-MEN-te.)

I would like to schedule an appointment with the doctor.
Gostaria de marcar uma consulta com o médico.
(gos-ta-REE-ah di MAR-kar OO-ma kon-SUL-ta kohm o MEE-dee-koh.)

I'm feeling quite unwell.
Estou me sentindo muito mal.
(es-TOH meh sen-TEEN-do MOY-toh mahl.)

I need a check-up.
Preciso de uma avaliação médica.
(pre-SEE-doh di OO-ma a-va-lee-ya-SAWN MEE-di-kah.)

I have some concerns about my health.
Tenho algumas preocupações com minha saúde.
(TEN-yoh al-GOO-mas pre-o-koo-pa-SAWNS kohm MEE-nya SAU-de.)

I've been experiencing some pain in my [body part].
Tenho sentido dor em minha [parte do corpo].
(TEN-yoh sen-TEEDOH dor em MEE-nya [PAR-teh do KOOR-po].)

I need a referral to see a specialist.
Preciso de uma indicação para um especialista.
(pre-SEE-doh di OO-ma een-dee-ka-SAWN pa-rah oom es-pe-shee-ah-LEES-ta.)

I'm here for a follow-up appointment.
Estou aqui para uma consulta de acompanhamento.
(es-TOH ah-KEE pa-rah OO-ma kon-SUL-ta di a-kom-pa-NYA-men-to.)

I'm here for a second opinion.
Estou aqui para uma segunda opinião.
(es-TOH ah-KEE pa-rah OO-ma se-goon-da oh-pee-NYAWN.)

I need to renew my prescription.
Preciso renovar minha receita.
(pre-SEE-doh reh-noh-VAHR MEE-nya reh-SEY-ta.)

I'm allergic to [medication/food] and need to avoid it.
Sou alérgico*(a)* a [medicamento/comida] e preciso evitá-lo*(a)*.
*(sow a-LEYR-ji-ko(a) a [meh-dee-ka-MEN-too/koh-MEE-da] e
pre-SEE-doh eh-vee-TAH-lo(a).)*

I've been feeling tired and rundown lately.
Tenho me sentido cansado e desgastado ultimamente.
*(TEN-yoh meh sen-TEEDOH kahn-SAH-doh ee des-gah-STAH-doh
ul-ti-ma-MEN-te.)*

I need to discuss my test results with the doctor.
Preciso discutir meus resultados de exames com o médico.
*(pre-SEE-doh dis-koo-TEER MAYS reh-sool-TA-dos di eh-KSA-mes kohm
o MEE-dee-koh.)*

I'm having trouble sleeping.
Estou tendo dificuldades para dormir.
(es-TOH TEN-doh dee-fee-kool-DAH-dees pah-rah dor-MEER.)

I need a flu shot or other vaccine.
Preciso de uma vacina contra a gripe ou outra vacina.
*(pre-SEE-doh di OO-ma va-SEE-nah kohn-tra a GREE-pee oh OH-tra
va-SEE-nah.)*

I'm pregnant and need to discuss my prenatal care.
Estou grávida e preciso discutir meu cuidado pré-natal.
*(es-TOH GRA-vee-dah ee pre-SEE-doh dis-koo-TEER MEE-oo
koo-ee-DAW pre-na-TAHL.)*

I've been experiencing some side effects from my medication.
Tenho tido alguns efeitos colaterais do meu medicamento.
(TEN-yoh TEE-doh AL-guns eh-FEI-tos ko-la-te-RAYS doo MEH-oo meh-dee-ka-MEN-to.)

I need a physical exam.
Preciso de um exame físico.
(pre-SEE-doh di oom eh-KSA-mee FEE-see-koo.)

I'm experiencing some mental health issues.
Estou tendo alguns problemas de saúde mental.
(es-TOH TEN-doh AL-guns pro-BLE-mas di SAU-de men-TAL.)

I have a family history of [condition] and need to be screened.
Tenho histórico familiar de [condição] e preciso ser avaliado.
(TEN-yoh his-TO-ree-koo fa-mee-LYAR di [kon-dih-SAWN] ee pre-SEE-doh ser ah-va-lee-AH-do.)

I need to schedule a blood test or other lab work.
Preciso agendar um exame de sangue ou outro teste de laboratório.
(pre-SEE-doh a-jen-DAHR oom eh-KSA-mee di SAN-gwe oh OH-troh TEH-sti di la-bo-ra-TOR-yoo.)

I need a referral for physical therapy or other treatment.
Preciso de uma indicação para fisioterapia ou outro tratamento.
(pre-SEE-doh di OO-ma een-dee-ka-SAWN pa-rah fee-zee-oh-teh-RAH-pee-ah oh OH-troh tra-ta-MEN-toh.)

I need a note for work or school.
Preciso de uma atestado para o trabalho ou a escola.
(pre-SEE-doh di OO-ma ah-tes-TA-do pa-rah o tra-BA-lyoo oh ah es-KOH-la.)

I need to discuss my diet and nutrition with the doctor.
Preciso discutir minha dieta e nutrição com o médico.
(pre-SEE-doh dis-koo-TEER MEE-nya dee-eh-ta ee noo-tree-SAWN kohm o MEE-dee-koh.)

I need to have my blood pressure checked.
Preciso ter minha pressão arterial verificada.
(pre-SEE-doh ter MEE-nya preh-SAW ahr-tee-ree-AWL
veh-ree-fee-KAH-dah.)

I have a cough or sore throat.
Estou com tosse ou dor de garganta.
(es-TOH kohm TAW-see oh dor di gar-GAHN-tah.)

I have a fever or other flu-like symptoms.
Tenho febre ou outros sintomas semelhantes aos da gripe.
(TEN-yoh FEH-breh oh OH-trohs sin-TOH-mahs se-mel-YAHN-tays
ah-oos dah GREE-pee.)

I need a prescription for a medication.
Preciso de uma receita médica para um medicamento.
(pre-SEE-doh di OO-ma heh-see-tah MEH-dee-kah pa-rah oom
meh-dee-ka-MEN-toh.)

I have an appointment with the doctor.
Eu tenho uma consulta com o médico.
(ayoo TEN-yoo OO-ma kohn-SOOL-tah kohm ooh MEH-dee-koh.)

GOING TO A DENTIST

I have an appointment with Dr. _____.
Eu tenho uma consulta com o Dr. _____.
(EH-oo TEH-nyoo OO-mah kohn-SOOL-tah kohm oh Doh-tohrr _____.)

I'm here for my dental checkup.
Eu estou aqui para minha consulta dentária.
(EH-oo EH-stoh AH-kee pah-rah MEE-nyah kohn-SOOL-tah dehn-TAH-ree-ah.)

I need to schedule a cleaning.
Eu preciso agendar uma limpeza.
(EH-oo preh-SEE-doh ah-gehN-DAHR OO-mah leem-PEH-zah.)

I have a toothache.
Eu estou com dor de dente.
(EH-oo EH-stoh kohm DOHR deh DEHN-teh.)

I'm experiencing sensitivity in my teeth.
Estou sentindo sensibilidade nos meus dentes.
(EH-stoh sehn-TEEN-doh sehn-see-bee-lee-DAH-deh nohs MEH-oos DEHN-tes.)

I broke a tooth and need it repaired.
Eu quebrei um dente e preciso consertá-lo.
(EH-oo keh-BREH-ee oong DEN-teh e preh-SEE-doh kohn-sehr-TAH-loh.)

I lost a filling and need it replaced.
Eu perdi uma obturação e preciso trocá-la.
(EH-oo PEHR-dee OO-mah ohb-too-rah-SOW oh preh-SEE-doh TROH-kah-lah.)

I have a cavity that needs to be filled.
Eu tenho uma cárie que precisa ser preenchida.
*(EH-oo TEH-nyoo OO-mah KAH-ree eh pree-SEE-zah sehr
preh-en-CHEE-dah.)*

I need a dental X-ray.
Eu preciso de um raio-x dentário.
(EH-oo preh-SEE-doh deh oong HAI-oh-shee DEHN-tah-ree-oh.)

I'm interested in teeth whitening.
Eu estou interessado em clareamento dental.
*(EH-stoh ehn-teh-RESS-ah-doh ehm klah-ree-AH-mehn-toh
dehn-TAH-lee.)*

Can you recommend a good toothpaste?
Você pode recomendar uma boa pasta de dente?
*(Voh-SEH poh-dee reh-koh-mehn-DAHR OO-mah BO-ah PAH-stah deh
DEHN-teh?)*

How often should I floss?
Com que frequência devo usar o fio dental?
(KOM keh freh-KWEHN-see-ah DEH-voh oo-ZAHR o FEE-oh DEHN-tahl?)

Do you have any tips for improving my dental hygiene?
Você tem alguma dica para melhorar minha higiene dental?
*(Voh-SEH tehm ahl-GOO-mah DEE-kah pah-rah meh-lyoh-RAHR
MEH-ooh-HEE-jee-neh DEHN-tahl?)*

How long will the procedure take?
Quanto tempo levará o procedimento?
(KWAN-too TEHM-poo leh-vah-RAH oh proh-seh-DEE-mehn-toh?)

Will I need any anesthesia?
Eu vou precisar de anestesia?
(EH-oo voh preh-SEE-doh deh ah-neh-steh-ZEE-ah?)

How much will the procedure cost?
Quanto custará o procedimento?
(KWAN-too koos-TAH-rah oh proh-seh-DEE-mehn-toh?)

101

Do you accept insurance?
Vocês aceitam seguro?
(Voh-SEHSS ah-seh-TAHM seh-GOO-roh?)

Can you explain the procedure to me?
Você pode explicar o procedimento para mim?
(Voh-SEH poh-dee ehks-plee-KAHR oh proh-seh-DEE-mehn-toh pah-rah meh?)

Is there any discomfort associated with the procedure?
Há algum desconforto associado ao procedimento?
(AH ahl-goom deh-shkohn-FOR-too ah-soh-see-AH-doh ah-oo proh-seh-DEE-mehn-toh?)

How long will it take for me to recover?
Quanto tempo levará para eu me recuperar?
(KWAN-too TEHM-poo leh-vah-RAH pah-rah EH-oo meh reh-koo-peh-RAHR?)

Can I eat or drink anything before the procedure?
Posso comer ou beber algo antes do procedimento?
(POH-soh koh-MEHR oh bee-BEHR AHL-goh AN-tehs doh proh-seh-DEE-mehn-toh?)

Will I need someone to drive me home after the procedure?
Eu precisarei de alguém para me levar para casa após o procedimento?
(EH-oo preh-SEE-deh-REE deh ahl-gyehm pah-rah meh leh-VAHR pah-rah KA-sah ah-Pohs oh proh-seh-DEE-mehn-toh?)

Will I need to take any medication after the procedure?
Eu precisarei tomar algum medicamento depois do procedimento?
(EH-oo preh-SEE-deh-REE toh-MAHR AHL-goom meh-dee-kah-MEN-toh DEH-poh-eez doh proh-seh-DEE-mehn-toh?)

Can you give me a prescription for pain medication?
Você pode me dar uma receita para medicamento para dor?
(Voh-SEH poh-dee meh dah OOH-mah reh-SEH-tah pah-rah meh-dee-kah-MEN-toh pah-rah dohr?)

How often should I come in for a checkup?
Com que frequência devo voltar para um checkup?
*(KOM keh freh-KWEHN-see-ah DEH-voh VOHL-tah pah-rah ooh
CHEH-kuhp?)*

Can you recommend any oral hygiene products?
Você pode me recomendar algum produto de higiene oral?
*(Voh-SEH poh-dee meh reh-koh-mehn-DAHR ahl-GOOM proh-DOO-toh
deh ee-zhee-EH-neh oh-RAHL?)*

Can you show me how to properly brush and floss my teeth?
Você pode me mostrar como escovar e usar o fio dental
corretamente?
*(Voh-SEH poh-dee meh mohs-TRAHR koh-moh es-KOH-vahr ee
oo-SAHR oh FEE-oh den-TAHL ko-rreh-ta-MEHN-teh?)*

Do you have any aftercare instructions for me?
Você tem alguma instrução pós-operatória para me dar?
*(Voh-SEH tehm ahl-GOO-mah een-stroo-SOW pohs
oh-peh-rah-TOH-ree-ah pah-rah meh DAHR?)*

Can you schedule my next appointment?
Você pode marcar minha próxima consulta?
*(Voh-SEH poh-dee mar-KAHR MEE-nah PROH-shee-mah
kohn-SOOL-tah?)*

Thank you, see you next time.
Obrigado, até a próxima.
(oh-bree-GAH-doh, ah-teh ah PROH-shee-mah.)

GIVING & RECEIVING DIRECTIONS

Insert the destination, if applicable.

Go straight ahead.
Siga em frente.
(SEE-gah ehm FREN-chee.)

Turn left at the traffic light.
Vire à esquerda no semáforo.
(VEE-reh ah ehs-KEHR-dah noh seh-MAH-foh-roh.)

Turn right at the intersection.
Vire à direita no cruzamento.
(VEE-reh ah dee-REI-tah noh kroo-zah-MEN-toh.)

Take the first/second/third street on the left/right.
Pegue a primeira/segunda/terceira rua à esquerda/direita.
(PEH-goo ah pree-MEI-rah/ seh-GOON-dah/ tehr-SEI-rah roo-ah ah ehs-KEHR-dah/dei-REI-tah.)

Go past the park/museum/library.
Passe pelo parque/museu/biblioteca.
(PAH-seh peh-loh PAHR-keh/moo-SEH-oo/bee-blee-oh-TEH-kah.)

It's on your left/right.
Está à sua esquerda/direita.
(EH-stah ah SOO-ah ehs-KEHR-dah/dei-REI-tah.)

You'll see a big sign that says…
Você verá uma placa grande que diz…
(VOH-seh veh-RAH OO-mah PLAH-kah GRAHN-dee keh deez.)

Keep going until you reach…
Continue até chegar em...
(KOHN-ti-noo ah-TEH cheh-GAHR ehm...)

You're going the wrong way.

Você está indo na direção errada.

(VOH-seh EH-stah EEN-doh nah dee-reh-SOWN eh-RAH-dah.)

You need to make a U-turn.

Você precisa fazer um retorno.

(VOH-seh PREH-see-sah fah-zer oom reh-TOR-noh.)

Take the highway/expressway/turnpike.

Pegue a rodovia/autoestrada/pedágio.

(PEH-goo ah roh-doh-VEE-ah/OW-too-es-TRAH-dah/peh-DAH-zhoh.)

Follow the signs for the airport/downtown.

Siga as placas para o aeroporto/centro da cidade.

(SEE-gah ahs PLAH-kahs PAH-rah oh EH-roh-POHR-toh/SEN-troh dah SEE-dah-deh.)

Take the second exit on the roundabout.

Pegue a segunda saída na rotatória.

(PEH-goo ah seh-GOON-dah SAH-ee-dah nah roh-tah-TOH-ree-ah.)

Keep going until you see the stop sign.

Continue até ver a placa de pare.

(KOHN-ti-noo ah-TEH vehr ah PLAH-kah deh PAH-reh.)

It's about a mile/kilometer down the road.

É cerca de uma milha/quilômetro adiante.

(EH SEHR-kah deh OO-mah MEE-lyah/kee-loh-MEH-troh ah-dyahN-teh.)

Turn left/right at the traffic light.

Vire à esquerda/direita no semáforo.

(VEE-reh ah ehs-KEHR-dah/dei-REI-tah noh seh-MAH-foh-roo.)

Go straight until you reach the intersection.

Siga em frente até chegar ao cruzamento.

(SEE-gah ehm FREHN-teh ah-TEH cheh-GAHR ow kroo-zah-MEN-too.)

You'll need to make a U-turn.
Você precisará fazer um retorno.
(VOH-seh preh-see-sah-RAH fah-ZEHR oom reh-TOHR-noo.)

Can you tell me how to get to [destination]?
Você pode me dizer como chegar em [destination]?
(vo-SE po-DE me di-ZER co-MO che-GAR em [ ]?)

Excuse me, do you know the way to [destination]?
Com licença, você sabe como chegar em [destination]?
(com li-SEN-ça, vo-CÊ SA-be co-MO che-GAR em [ ]?)

Could you point me in the direction of [destination]?
Você poderia me indicar a direção de [destination]?
(vo-SE po-de-RIA me in-di-CAR a di-re-ÇÃO de [ ]?)

I'm trying to find my way to [destination], can you help me?
Estou tentando encontrar o caminho para [destination], você pode me ajudar?
(es-TOU ten-TAN-do en-CON-trar o ca-MI-nho pa-RA [des-ti-NA-tion], vo-CÊ po-de me a-JU-dar?)

Which way should I go to get to [destination]?
Que caminho devo seguir para chegar em [destination]?
(que ca-MI-nho DE-vo se-GUIR pa-ra che-GAR em [ ]?)

Is [destination] nearby? How do I get there?
[destination] fica perto daqui? Como faço para chegar lá?
([des-ti-NA-tion] FI-ca PER-to da-QUI? CO-mo FA-ço pa-ra che-GAR lá?)

Would you be able to give me directions to [destination]?
Você poderia me dar as instruções para chegar em [destination]?
(vo-SE po-de-RIA me dar as ins-tru-ÇÕES pa-ra che-GAR em [ ]?)

Can you show me how to get to [destination] on a map?
Você pode me mostrar como chegar em [destination] em um mapa?
(vo-SE po-de me mos-TRAR co-MO che-GAR em [des-ti-NA-tion] em um MA-pa?)

I'm a bit lost, can you help me find my way to [destination]?
Estou um pouco perdido, você pode me ajudar a encontrar o caminho para [destination]?
(es-TOU um PO-co per-DI-do, vo-CÊ po-de me a-JU-dar a en-CON-trar o ca-MI-nho pa-ra [ ]?)

How far is [destination] from here and how do I get there?
Qual a distância de [destination] daqui e como chego lá?
(qual a dis-TÂN-cia de [des-ti-NA-tion] da-QUI e CO-mo che-go lá?)

What's the best way to get to [destination]?
Qual é a melhor maneira de chegar em [destination]?
(qual é a ME-lhor ma-NEI-ra de che-GAR em [ ]?)

Is there a specific route I should take to get to [destination]?
Existe uma rota específica que eu devo seguir para chegar em [destination]?
(e-xis-te u-ma RO-ta es-pe-CÍ-fi-ca que eu DE-vo se-GUIR pa-ra che-GAR em [ ]?)

Can you give me step-by-step directions to [destination]?
Você pode me dar as direções passo a passo para chegar em [destination]?
(vo-SE po-de me dar as di-re-ÇÕES PAS-so a PAS-so pa-ra che-GAR em [ ]?)

I'm not familiar with the area, can you guide me to [destination]?
Eu não estou familiarizado com a área, você pode me guiar até [destination]?
(eu não es-TOU fa-mi-li-a-ri-ZA-do com a Á-rea, vo-CÊ po-de me gui-AR até [ ]?)

Can you tell me which street to turn onto to get to [destination]?
Você pode me dizer em qual rua eu devo virar para chegar em [destination]?
(vo-SE po-de me di-ZER em qual RU-a eu DE-vo vi-RAR pa-ra che-GAR em [ ]?)

Do I need to take any highways or main roads to get to [destination]?

Eu preciso pegar alguma rodovia ou estrada principal para chegar em [destination]?

(eu pre-CI-so pe-GAR al-GU-ma ro-do-VI-a ou es-tra-DA prin-ci-PAL pa-ra che-GAR em [ ]?)

Should I follow a particular landmark to get to [destination]?

Eu devo seguir algum ponto de referência específico para chegar em [destination]?

(eu DE-vo se-GUIR al-GUM pon-TO de re-fe-RÊN-cia es-pe-CÍ-fi-co pa-ra che-GAR em [ ]?)

Is it easy to find parking near [destination]?

É fácil encontrar estacionamento próximo de [destination]?

(é FÁ-cil en-CON-trar es-ta-ci-o-na-MEN-to PRÓ-xi-mo de [ ]?)

Is there a bus/train station near [destination] that I can take?

Existe uma estação de ônibus/trem perto de [destination] que eu possa pegar?

(e-xis-te u-ma es-ta-ÇÃO de ô-NI-bus/trem PER-to de [des-ti-NA-tion] que eu POS-sa pe-GAR?)

How long will it take me to get to [destination]?

Quanto tempo vai levar para eu chegar em [destination]?

(QUAN-to TEM-po VAI le-VAR pa-ra eu che-GAR em [ ]?)

Will I need to make any turns to get to [destination]?

Precisarei fazer alguma curva para chegar a [destination]?

(prey-see-ZAH-rey fah-ZER ah-GOO-mah KOOR-vah pah-RA che-GAR ah [ ]?)

Which direction should I head in to get to [destination]?

Em que direção devo ir para chegar a [destination]?

(eng KEE dee-reh-SHOW DEH-vo eer PAH-ra che-GAR ah [ ]?)

Can you give me some landmarks to look out for on my way to [destination]?
Você pode me dar algumas referências para eu observar no caminho até [destination]?
(voh-SEH poh-deh meh DAHR ah-GOO-mahs reh-feh-REN-see-as pah-RA eh-oo ob-ser-VAHR noh kah-MEE-nyoo ah-TEE [ ]?)

Are there any shortcuts or alternate routes to get to [destination]?
Existem atalhos ou rotas alternativas para chegar a [destination]?
(egs-ees-TEHM ah-TAH-lyoos oo RO-tas al-ter-NA-tee-vas PAH-ra che-GAR ah [ ]?)

Is there anything I should avoid on the way to [destination]?
Existe algo que eu deva evitar no caminho para [destination]?
(ehgs-SEES-teh AHL-go keh eh-OO DEH-vah eh-vee-TAR noh kah-MEE-nyoo PAH-ra [ ]?)

Do I need to take any ferries or bridges to get to [destination]?
Preciso pegar alguma balsa ou ponte para chegar a [destination]?
(prey-SEE-zoh peh-GAR AHL-goo-mah BAHLSAH oo PON-teh PAH-ra che-GAR ah [ ]?)

Will I pass any major intersections on my way to [destination]?
Passarei por alguma grande intersecção no caminho até [destination]?
(pah-sah-RAY poor AHL-goo-mah GRAHN-jee in-ter-seh-SOH noh kah-MEE-nyoo ah-TEE [ ]?)

Can you give me an idea of what the area around [destination] looks like?
Você pode me dar uma ideia de como é a área ao redor de [destination]?
(voh-SEH poh-deh meh DAHR OO-mah ee-DEH-yah deh KO-moh eh ah AH-ree-ah ow heh-DOR di [ ]?)

Can you tell me if there are any road closures or construction near [destination]?
Você pode me dizer se há algum fechamento de estrada ou construção perto de [destination]?
(voh-SEH poh-deh meh dee-ZEHR see ah AHL-goom feh-shah-MEN-toh deh es-TRAH-dah oo kon-stru-SOW pehr-toh di [ ]?)

Can you recommend the safest route to get to [destination]?
Você pode recomendar a rota mais segura para chegar ao [ ]?
*(voh-say poh-day reh-koh-mehn-DAHR ah ROH-tah mahys
seh-GOO-rah pah-rah cheh-GAHR oh [ ])*

COMMON QUESTIONS WHEN ARRIVING IN A NEW COUNTRY

What is the local currency and exchange rate?
Qual é a moeda local e taxa de câmbio?
(KAHL eh ah MOY-dah LOH-kahl ee TAH-kah deh KAHM-byo?)

Where is the nearest bank or ATM?
Onde fica o banco ou caixa eletrônico mais próximo?
(OHN-deh FEE-kah oh BAHN-koo oh KAH-shah eh-leh-TRAW-nee-koh mahys PROH-ksih-moh?)

What is the country's official language?
Qual é a língua oficial do país?
(KAHL eh ah LEEN-gwah oh-fee-SYAWL doo pah-EEZ?)

How do I get to my accommodation?
Como chego ao meu alojamento?
(KOH-moh CHEH-goh ow mayoo ah-loh-jah-MEN-too?)

What is the local transportation system like?
Como é o sistema de transporte local?
(KOH-moh eh oh sis-TEH-mah deh trahn-spohr-tchee LOH-kahl?)

Are there any cultural customs or practices that I should be aware of?
Existem costumes ou práticas culturais dos quais eu deveria estar ciente?
(eh-shish-TEHM kohs-TOO-mesh oh prah-TEE-kahsh kool-too-RAH-ees doosh kwah-ees ehoo deh-veh-REE-ah ehss-TAHR see-EN-teh?)

What are the local emergency numbers?
Quais são os números de emergência locais?
(kwah-ees SAH-ooh ohss NOO-meh-roosh deh eh-mehr-JEN-see-ah LOH-kah-ees?)

Is there a tourist information center nearby?
Existe algum centro de informações turísticas por perto?
(eh-SHEES-teh ah-GOOM SEHN-troo deh een-fohr-mah-SAWNS
too-ris-TEE-kahsh pohr PEHR-tooh?)

What are the local laws and regulations?
Quais são as leis e regulamentos locais?
(kwah-ees SAH-ooh ahs LEH-ees ee reh-goo-lah-MEN-toosh
LOH-kah-ees?)

How do I obtain a SIM card for my phone?
Como faço para obter um cartão SIM para meu celular?
(KOH-moh FASS-oh pah-rah ohb-TEHR oong kar-TAHW SIM pah-rah
mayoo seh-loo-LAHR?)

Are there any local festivals or events happening soon?
Existem festivais ou eventos locais acontecendo em breve?
(eh-shish-TEHM fes-tee-VAH-ee-oosh oh eh-vehn-toosh LOH-kah-ees
ah-kawn-TAY-sen-doh ehn BREH-veh?)

Where are the best places to eat or drink?
Onde estão os melhores lugares para comer ou beber?
(OHN-deh eh-STAH-ooh ohs meh-LYOH-reesh LUGAH-res pah-rah
KOH-mehr oo beh-BEHR?)

What are the must-see tourist attractions?
Quais são as atrações turísticas que não posso perder?
(kwah-ees SAH-ooh ahss ah-trah-SEE-ohneesh too-ree-STEEK-ahsh keh
nahw POH-soh PEHR-dehr?)

How do I say common phrases in the local language?
Como digo frases comuns no idioma local?
(KOH-moh DEE-goh FRAH-zesh koh-MOONSH noh ee-jee-OH-mah
LOH-kahl?)

Can you recommend any local attractions or activities?
Você pode recomendar alguma atração ou atividade local?
(voh-SAY poh-deh reh-koh-mehn-DAHR ah-GOO-mah ah-trah-SEE-own
oh ah-tee-VEE-dah-deh LOH-kahl?)

How much does public transportation cost?
Quanto custa o transporte público?
(KWAN-toh KOOS-tah oh trahn-spohr-tee poo-BLEE-koo?)

Can you recommend a good restaurant nearby?
Você pode recomendar um bom restaurante por perto?
*(voh-SAY poh-deh reh-koh-mehn-DAHR oong boh-ooh
res-taw-RAHN-chee pohr PEHR-tooh?)*

How do I connect to the internet?
Como me conecto à internet?
(KOH-moh meh kohn-EHK-tooh ah ehn-ter-NEHT?)

Are there any local customs or traditions I should be aware of?
Existem costumes ou tradições locais dos quais eu deveria estar
ciente?
*(eh-shish-TEHM kohs-TOO-mesh oh trah-dee-SAWNS LOH-kahl doh
kwah-ees ehoo deh-veh-REE-ah ehss-TAHR see-EN-teh?)*

Can you recommend a good place to shop?
Você pode recomendar um bom lugar para fazer compras?
*(voh-SAY poh-deh reh-koh-mehn-DAHR oong boh-ooh LOO-gahr
pah-rah FEH-zehr KOHM-prahsh?)*

Is it safe to walk around the area at night?
É seguro caminhar pela área à noite?
(eh seh-GOO-roh kah-mee-NYAR pee-lah AH-ree-ah ah NOY-chee?)

Where can I find a good pharmacy?
Onde posso encontrar uma boa farmácia?
*(OHN-deh POH-soh ehn-kohn-TRAHR OO-mah BOH-ah
fahr-MAH-see-ah?)*

Can you recommend a good place to stay?
Você pode recomendar um bom lugar para ficar?
*(voh-SAY poh-deh reh-koh-mehn-DAHR oong boh-ooh LOO-gahr
pah-rah FEE-kahr?)*

What is the weather like at this time of year?
Como está o clima nesta época do ano?
(KOH-moh ehs-TAH oh KLEE-mah NEHS-tah EHP-kah doo ahn-yoh?)

What is the local time?
Que horas são localmente?
(keh OH-rahsh sahw LOH-kahl-mehn-teh?)

How do I get a local phone number?
Como faço para obter um número de telefone local?
(KOH-mohfah-soh PAH-rah ohb-TEHR oong NOO-meh-roh deh teh-leh-FOH-neh LOH-kahl?)

Are there any local festivals or events happening soon?
Existem festivais ou eventos locais acontecendo em breve?
(eh-shis-TEHM fes-tee-VAH-ee-oosh oh ee-VEHN-toosh LOH-kahl-ees ah-kawn-TEH-see-EN-doh ehm BREH-veh?)

Can you recommend a good place to experience local cuisine?
Você pode recomendar um bom lugar para experimentar a culinária local?
(voh-SAY poh-deh reh-koh-mehn-DAHR oong boh-ooh LOO-gahr pah-rah ehks-peh-ree-men-TAHR ah koo-lee-NAH-ree-ah LOH-kahl?)

What are the emergency numbers in this country?
Quais são os números de emergência neste país?
(kwah-ees SAH-ooh ohsh NOO-meh-rohsh deh eh-mehr-JEN-see-ah NEHS-teh PAH-ee?)

Can you recommend a good local guide or tour company?
Você pode recomendar um bom guia local ou empresa de turismo?
(voh-SAY poh-deh reh-koh-mehn-DAHR oong boh-ooh GEE-ah LOH-kahl oh ehm-preh-zah deh too-REEZ-moh?)

BEING POLITE

Thank you
Obrigado
(oh-bree-GAH-doh)

Excuse me
Com licença
(cohm lee-SEN-sah)

Please
Por favor
(poor fah-VOHR)

Pardon me
Desculpe-me
(dehs-KOOL-peh meh)

May I
Posso
(POH-soh)

Could you
Você poderia
(voh-SEH poh-deh-REE-ah)

Would you mind
Você se importaria
(voh-SEH see ehm-por-tee-AH-ree-ah)

I'm sorry
Desculpe-me
(dehs-KOOL-peh meh)

After you
Depois de você
(deh-POYSH deh voh-SEH)

Go ahead
Adiante
(ah-dee-AHN-teh)

No problem
Sem problema
(sehn proh-BLEH-mah)

It was my pleasure
Foi um prazer
(foh-ee oong prah-ZEHR)

My apologies
Minhas desculpas
(MEE-nhahs dehs-KOOL-pahs)

With all due respect
Com todo o respeito
(cohm TOH-doh oh rehs-PEH-toh)

If you don't mind
Se você não se importa
(seh voh-SEH nãoh see ehm-por-tah)

If it's not too much trouble
Se não for pedir muito
(seh nãoh fohr peh-DEER MOO-ee-toh)

I beg your pardon
Peço desculpas
(PEH-soh dehs-KOOL-pahs)

Thank you kindly
Muito obrigado
(MOO-ee-toh oh-bree-GAH-doh)

You're welcome
De nada
(deh NAH-dah)

No, thank you
Não, obrigado
(nãoh oh-bree-GAH-doh)

After you, please
Depois de você, por favor
(deh-POYSH deh voh-SEH, poor fah-VOHR)

If I may ask
Se eu posso perguntar
(seh ehoo POH-soh per-GOON-tahr)

If I may add
Se eu posso acrescentar
(seh ehoo POH-soh ah-kreh-SEN-tahr)

Thank you for your time
Obrigado pelo seu tempo
(oh-bree-GAH-doh peh-loh seh-oo TEHM-poh)

It's been a pleasure
Foi um prazer
(foh-ee oong prah-ZEHR)

I appreciate it
Eu agradeço
(eh-oo ah-grah-DEH-soo)

If I can be of any assistance
Se eu puder ajudar em alguma coisa
(seh ehoo POO-dehr ah-zhoo-DAR ehn ahl-GOO-mah COY-sah)

I'll be happy to help
Ficarei feliz em ajudar
(fee-kah-RAY fee-LEEZ ehm ah-zhoo-DAHR)

That's very kind of you
Isso é muito gentil da sua parte
(EE-soh eh MOO-ee-toh jehn-TEEL dah soo-ah PAHR-chee)

Thank you in advance
Desde já agradeço
(DEHSH-deh JAH ah-grah-DEH-soo)

Excuse me for interrupting
Desculpe-me por interromper
(dehs-KOOL-peh meh pohr ehn-teh-rohm-PEHR)

I appreciate your help
Agradeço sua ajuda
(ah-grah-DEH-soh SOO-ah ah-ZHOO-dah)

Please let me know
Por favor, me avise
(poor fah-VOHR, meh ah-VEE-seh)

May I ask a question?
Posso fazer uma pergunta?
(POH-soh fah-ZEHR OO-mah pehr-GOON-tah?)

Could you repeat that, please?
Poderia repetir, por favor?
(poh-deh-REE-ah reh-peh-TEER, poor fah-VOHR?)

Would you be so kind as to...
Seria tão gentil de sua parte...
(SEH-ree-ah tahw jehn-TEEL deh SOO-ah PAHR-chee...)

I'm sorry to bother you
Desculpe-me incomodar
(dehs-KOOL-peh meh ehn-koh-moh-DAHR)

After you, please
Depois de você, por favor
(deh-POYSH deh voh-SEH, poor fah-VOHR)

Thank you for your understanding
Obrigado pela compreensão
(oh-bree-GAH-doh peh-lah kohm-preh-ehn-SAH-oo)

No, thank you, I'm good
Não, obrigado, estou bem
(não, oh-bree-GAH-doh, eh-stohh behn)

Please, take a seat
Por favor, sente-se
(poor fah-VOHR, SEHN-teh-seh)

I'll do my best
Vou fazer o meu melhor
(voh fah-ZEHR oh may-oo meh-LHOHR)

Thank you for your patience
Obrigado pela paciência
(oh-bree-GAH-doh peh-lah pah-see-EN-see-ah)

May I offer you something to drink?
Posso oferecer algo para beber?
(POH-soh oh-feh-REH-sehr AHL-goh pah-rah BEH-behr?)

Would you like me to help you?
Gostaria que eu o ajudasse?
(gohs-TAH-ree-ah keh ehoo oh ah-zhoo-DAHS-see?)

I beg your pardon, I didn't catch that
Peço desculpas, não entendi
(PEH-soh dehs-KOOL-pahs, nãoh ehn-TEN-dee)

If it's not too much trouble
Se não for incômodo
(seh nãoh fohr een-KOH-moh-doh)

Thank you for your hospitality
Obrigado pela hospitalidade
(oh-bree-GAH-doh peh-lah oh-spee-tah-lee-DAH-deh)

That's very generous of you
Isso é muito generoso de sua parte
(EE-soh eh MOO-ee-toh jeh-neh-ROH-soo deh SOO-ah PAHR-chee)

Please accept my apologies
Por favor, aceite minhas desculpas
(poor fah-VOHR, ah-SEH-teh MEE-nhahs deh-SKOO-lpahs)

If I may make a suggestion
Se me permite fazer uma sugestão
(seh meh pehr-MEE-teh fah-ZEHR OO-mah soo-zheh-STAHW)

I'm sorry, I didn't mean to
Desculpe, não foi minha intenção
(dehs-KOOL-peh, nãoh foh-ee MEE-nhah een-tehn-SAHW)

Thank you for taking the time
Obrigado por ter dedicado seu tempo
(oh-bree-GAH-doh pohr teh-ehr deh-dee-KAH-doh SOO-ah TEHM-poh)

May I offer you a hand?
Posso lhe dar uma mão?
(POH-soh lee Dahr OO-mah MAH-oh?)

My apologies for the inconvenience
Minhas desculpas pelo incômodo
(MEE-nhahs deh-SKOO-lpahs peh-loh een-KOH-moh-doh)

Please forgive me
Por favor, me perdoe
(poor fah-VOHR, meh pehr-DOH-eh)

I really appreciate it
Eu realmente agradeço
(ehoo reh-ahl-mehn-tee ah-grah-DEH-soo)

Thank you for your time and attention
Obrigado pelo seu tempo e atenção
(oh-bree-GAH-doh peh-loh seh-oo TEHM-poh ee ah-ten-SAHW)

It was nice meeting you
Foi um prazer conhecê-lo
(foy oongh PRAH-zehr kohn-yeh-SEH-loh)

Excuse me, would you happen to know...?
Com licença, você saberia...?
(kohm lee-SEHN-sah, voh-SEH sah-beh-REE-ah...?)

DESCRIBING PEOPLE

Confident
Confidente
(kohn-fee-DEHN-teh)

Cautious
Cauteloso
(kow-teh-LOH-soo)

Brave
Corajoso
(koh-rah-JOH-soo)

Fearful
Temeroso
(teh-meh-ROH-soo)

Careless
Descuidado
(dehs-koo-ee-DAH-doo)

Meticulous
Minucioso
(mee-noo-SEE-oh-soo)

Energetic
Energético
(eh-ner-JEH-tee-koh)

Laid-back
Relaxado
(reh-lah-SHAH-doo)

Creative
Criativo
(kree-ah-TEE-vooh)

Logical
Lógico
(LOH-jee-koh)

Ambitious
Ambicioso
(ahm-bee-SYO-soo)

Humble
Humilde
(oo-MEEL-deh)

Arrogant
Arrogante
(ah-roh-GAHN-teh)

Thoughtful
Pensativo
(pehn-sah-TEE-voh)

Impulsive
Impulsivo
(eem-POOL-see-voh)

Patient
Paciente
(pah-see-EHN-teh)

Impatient
Impaciente
(eem-pah-see-EHN-teh)

Sociable
Sociável
(soh-see-AH-vehl)

Reserved
Reservado
(reh-zehr-VAH-doo)

Reliable
Confiável
(kohn-fee-AH-vehl)

Unreliable
Não confiável
(now kohn-fee-AH-vehl)

Diligent
Diligente
(dee-lee-JEHN-teh)

Lazy
Preguiçoso
(preh-gwee-SOH-soo)

Outgoing
Extrovertido
(ehks-troh-vehr-TEE-doo)

Introverted
Introvertido
(een-troh-vehr-TEE-doo)

Impressive
Impressionante
(eem-preh-syoh-NAHN-teh)

Mediocre
Medíocre
(meh-DEE-oh-kreh)

Enthusiastic
Entusiasmado
(ehn-too-zee-AH-mah-doo)

Lackadaisical
Desleixado
(dehs-leh-SHAH-doo)

Punctual
Pontual
(pohn-choo-AHL)

MAKING SUGGESTIONS

How about we...
Que tal nós...
(keh TAH-oo nohs...)

Why don't we...
Por que não nós...
(pohr kee nah-oo nohs...)

Have you considered...
Você já considerou...
(voh-SEH jah con-sih-deh-ROH-oo...)

Maybe we could...
Talvez nós possamos...
(tahl-VEHZ nohs poh-SAH-moos...)

Would you like to...
Você gostaria de...
(voh-SEH goh-stah-REE-ah deh...)

It might be a good idea to...
Pode ser uma boa ideia...
(POH-deh sehr OO-mah boh-ah ee-DEH-ah...)

I suggest that we...
Eu sugiro que nós...
(eh-oo soo-GHEE-roh keh nohs...)

EXPRESSING OPINIONS

In my opinion...
Na minha opinião...
(NA MEE-nha oh-pee-NYOW)

I believe that...
Eu acredito que...
(eh-YOO ah-kreh-DEE-toh keh...)

From my point of view...
Do meu ponto de vista...
(duh MEH-ooh POHN-toh deh VEE-stah...)

Personally, I think that...
Pessoalmente, eu acho que...
(peh-soo-AHL-men-teh, eh-YOO ah-SHOO keh...)

TALKING ABOUT HOBBIES AND INTERESTS

I enjoy playing video games.
Eu gosto de jogar VIDEOGAMES.
(ehu goh-stoh djoh-GAHR vee-duh-GAYMS)

My favorite hobby is reading books.
Meu hobby favorito é ler LIVROS.
(meh-oo HOH-bee fah-voh-REE-too eh lehr LEE-vroos)

I like to go for long walks in nature.
Eu gosto de fazer LONGAS CAMINHADAS na natureza.
(ehu goh-stoh djee FEH-zer LOHNG-gahs kah-mee-NYAH-dahs nah nah-too-REH-zah)

I enjoy watching movies and TV shows.
Eu gosto de assistir FILMES e programas de TV.
(ehu goh-stoh djee ah-see-STHEER FEE-mes ee proh-grah-mahs djee TV)

My favorite hobby is photography.
Meu hobby favorito é FOTOGRAFIA.
(meh-oo HOH-bee fah-voh-REE-too eh foh-toh-grah-FEE-ah)

I love listening to music and attending concerts.
Eu adoro ouvir MÚSICA e ir a CONCERTOS.
(ehu ah-DOH-roh oh-VEER MOO-see-kah ee eer ah koh-NEHR-toos)

I enjoy cooking and trying new recipes.
Eu gosto de cozinhar e experimentar NOVAS RECEITAS.
(ehu goh-stoh djee koh-zee-NYAH ehe eks-peh-ree-men-TAHR NOH-vahs reh-seh-EE-tahs)

I like to travel and explore new places.
Eu gosto de viajar e explorar NOVOS LUGARES.
*(ehu goh-stoh djee vyah-JAHR ehe eks-ploh-RAHR NO-vohs
loo-GAH-rehs)*

My favorite hobby is painting and drawing.
Meu hobby favorito é PINTURA e desenho.
*(meh-oo HOH-bee fah-voh-REE-too eh peen-TOO-rah ee
deh-SEHN-yoo)*

I love playing musical instruments.
Eu amo tocar INSTRUMENTOS MUSICIAIS.
(ehu AH-moh toh-KAHR een-stroo-men-TOOS moo-zee-kah-EYS)

I enjoy gardening and growing my own vegetables.
Eu gosto de jardinagem e cultivar MINHAS PRÓPRIAS VERDURAS.
*(ehu goh-stoh djee jahr-dee-NAH-jem ee kool-tee-VAHR MEE-nhas
PRO-pree-ahs vehr-DOO-ras)*

I like to do DIY projects around the house.
Eu gosto de fazer projetos faça-você-mesmo em CASA.
*(ehu goh-stoh djee FEH-zer proh-jeh-tos FAH-sah-VOH-see-moo ehn
KAH-sah)*

My favorite hobby is playing sports, especially soccer.
Meu hobby favorito é jogar ESPORTES, especialmente futebol.
*(meh-oo HOH-bee fah-voh-REE-too eh djoh-GAHR ess-POHR-tes,
espeh-tsyahl-mehn-teh foo-teh-BOOL)*

I love to dance and take dance classes.
Eu adoro dançar e fazer aulas de dança.
(ehu ah-DOH-roh dahn-SAHR ehe FEH-zer OW-lahs djee DAHN-sah)

I enjoy writing and journaling.
Eu gosto de escrever e fazer DIÁRIOS.
(ehu goh-stoh djee es-kreh-VEHR ehe FEH-zer dee-AH-ree-oos)

My favorite hobby is watching and analyzing sports games.
Meu hobby favorito é assistir e analisar jogos de ESPORTE.
(meh-oo HOH-bee fah-voh-REE-too eh ah-see-STHEER ee ah-nah-lee-ZAHR JOH-gos djee ess-POHR-teh)

I like to collect stamps and coins.
Eu gosto de colecionar SELOS e moedas.
(ehu goh-stoh djee koh-leh-see-oh-NAHR SEH-loos ee MOY-dahs)

I enjoy going to the gym and working out.
Eu gosto de ir à ACADEMIA e fazer EXERCÍCIOS.
(ehu goh-stoh djee eer ah ah-kah-DEH-mee-ah ehe FEH-zer ehk-sehr-SEE-syohs)

I like to go fishing and camping.
Eu gosto de pescar e acampar.
(ehu goh-stoh djee peh-SKAHR ee ah-kahm-PAHR)

My favorite hobby is playing board games with friends.
Meu hobby favorito é jogar jogos de TABULEIRO com amigos.
(meh-oo HOH-bee fah-voh-REE-too eh djoh-GAHR JOH-gos djee tah-boo-LEH-roh kohm ah-MEE-gohs)

I love to go to the theater and see live performances.
Eu adoro ir ao TEATRO e assistir apresentações ao vivo.
(ehu ah-DOH-roh eer ah-OH teh-AH-troh ee ah-see-STHEER ah-preh-sen-tah-SEE-ohs ah-oh VEE-voh)

I enjoy attending art exhibitions and museums.
Eu gosto de ir a exposições de arte e MUSEUS.
(ehu goh-stoh djee eer ah ehks-poh-see-SOH-ees djee AH-rteh ee moo-ZE-oos)

My favorite hobby is practicing yoga and meditation.
Meu hobby favorito é praticar YOGA e meditação.
(meh-oo HOH-bee fah-voh-REE-too eh prah-TEE-kahr YOH-gah ehe meh-dee-tah-SEE-oh)

I like to do crossword puzzles and other brain teasers.
Eu gosto de fazer palavras cruzadas e outros DESAFIOS MENTAIS.
(ehu goh-stoh djee FEH-zer pah-LAH-vrahs KROO-zah-dahs ee OH-troos deh-sah-FEE-ohs mehn-TAH-ys)

I love to read and write poetry.
Eu amo ler e escrever poesia.
(ehu AH-moh lehr ehe es-kreh-VEHR poh-eh-ZEE-ah)

My favorite hobby is woodworking and carpentry.
Meu hobby favorito é marcenaria e carpintaria.
(meh-oo HOH-bee fah-voh-REE-too eh mahr-seh-NAH-ree-ah ehe kahr-pin-TAH-ree-ah)

I like to go to the beach and spend time by the water.
Eu gosto de ir à praia e passar tempo perto da água.
(ehu goh-stoh djee eer ah PRAH-ee-ah e pass-AHR TEHM-poh PEHR-too dah AH-gwah)

I enjoy playing chess and other strategy games.
Eu gosto de jogar xadrez e outros jogos de ESTRATÉGIA.
(ehu goh-stoh djee djoh-GAHR SHA-drehs ee OH-troos JOH-gos djee ess-trah-TEH-zhee-ah)

My favorite hobby is birdwatching and observing wildlife.
Meu hobby favorito é observação de aves e vida selvagem.
(meh-oo HOH-bee fah-voh-REE-too eh ohb-ser-vah-SOW djee AH-vehz e VEED-ah sehl-VAH-zhehng)

I enjoy attending festivals and cultural events.
Eu gosto de participar de festivais e eventos culturais.
(ehu goh-stoh djee pahr-tee-pee-AHR djee fes-tee-VAH-ees ee eh-VEHN-toos kool-too-RAH-ee-ahs)

I love to go to amusement parks and ride roller coasters.
Eu amo ir a parques de diversões e andar em montanhas-russas.
(ehu AH-moh eer ah PAHR-kees djee dee-vehr-SOHNS ee ahn-DAHR ehm mohn-tah-NYAH-roo-sahs)

My favorite hobby is collecting vinyl records.

Meu hobby favorito é colecionar discos de vinil.

(meh-oo HOH-bee fah-voh-REE-too eh koh-leh-see-oh-NAHR DEE-skohs djee vee-NEEL)

I like to go on long road trips and explore new places.

Eu gosto de fazer viagens de carro longas e explorar novos lugares.

(ehu goh-stoh djee FAH-zer vee-AH-jens djee KAH-roh LOHNG-gahs ee ehks-ploh-RAHR NOH-voos LOO-gah-rehs)

I enjoy hiking and camping in the mountains.

Eu gosto de caminhar e acampar nas montanhas.

(ehu goh-stoh djee kah-mee-NYAH e ah-kahm-PAHR nahs mohn-tah-NYAHs)

My favorite hobby is baking and trying new dessert recipes.

Meu hobby favorito é assar e experimentar novas receitas de sobremesa.

(meh-oo HOH-bee fah-voh-REE-too eh ah-SAH ehe eks-peh-ree-men-TAHR NOH-vahs reh-SEH-tahs djee soh-BREH-meh-sah)

I like to practice meditation and mindfulness.

Eu gosto de praticar meditação e mindfulness.

(ehu goh-stoh djee prah-tee-KAHR meh-dee-tah-SOW ehe meen-FUHL-nehs)

I love to go to the zoo and see all the animals.

Eu amo ir ao zoológico e ver todos os animais.

(ehu AH-moh eer ah-zoo-loh-JEE-koh ehe vehr TOH-doos oh ah-nee-MAH-ee-oos)

My favorite hobby is studying different languages.

Meu hobby favorito é estudar diferentes idiomas.

(meh-oo HOH-bee fah-voh-REE-too eh ehs-too-DAHR dee-fee-REHN-tees ee-jjah-MOHS)

I enjoy watching documentaries and learning new things.
Eu gosto de assistir documentários e aprender coisas novas.
*(ehu goh-stoh djee ah-see-STEER doh-kooh-men-TAH-ree-oos ee
ah-prehn-DEHR KOH-zahs NOH-voos)*

I like to practice yoga and Pilates for exercise.
Eu gosto de praticar yoga e Pilates para exercício.
*(ehu goh-stoh djee prah-tee-KAHR YOH-gah ehe pee-LAH-tess pah-rah
ehks-ehr-SEE-see-oh)*

I enjoy going to concerts and listening to live music.
Eu gosto de ir a shows e ouvir música ao vivo.
*(ehu goh-stoh djee eer ah SHOWS ee oh-VEER MOO-zee-kah ah-o
VEE-voh)*

My favorite hobby is doing puzzles and brain teasers.
Meu hobby favorito é fazer quebra-cabeças e desafios mentais.
*(meh-oo HOH-bee fah-voh-REE-too eh fah-ZEHR KEH-brah-KAH-siss ee
deh-sah-FEE-ohs mehn-TAH-ee-ss)*

I like to go on bike rides and explore new trails.
Eu gosto de fazer passeios de bicicleta e explorar novas trilhas.
*(ehu goh-stoh djee FAH-zer pah-SEH-ohs djee bee-see-KLEH-tah ee
ehks-ploh-RAHR NOH-vaiss TREE-lhas)*

I love to read and watch sci-fi and fantasy movies.
Eu amo ler e assistir filmes de ficção científica e fantasia.
*(ehu AH-moh lehr ee ah-see-STEEHR FEE-mess djee fee-KSAW
syehn-TEEF-ikah ee fahn-TAH-zee-ah)*

My favorite hobby is playing video games with friends.
Meu hobby favorito é jogar videogames com amigos.
*(meh-oo HOH-bee fah-voh-REE-too eh joh-GAHR vee-deh-oh-GAH-mess
kohm ah-MEE-gohs)*

I like to go to the park and have picnics with my family.
Eu gosto de ir ao parque e fazer piqueniques com minha família.
*(ehu goh-stoh djee eer ah-oo PAHR-keh ee fah-ZEHR pee-keh-NEE-kees
kohm MEE-nhah fah-MEE-lyah)*

I enjoy playing board games and card games.
Eu gosto de jogar jogos de tabuleiro e jogos de cartas.
(ehu goh-stoh djee joh-GAHR JOH-gohs djee tah-boo-LEH-roo ee JOH-gohs djee KAHR-tahs)

My favorite hobby is watching the sunset and taking photographs.
Meu hobby favorito é assistir o pôr do sol e tirar fotografias.
(meh-oo HOH-bee fah-voh-REE-too eh ah-see-STEEHR oh POR doh SOHL ee chee-RAHR foh-toh-grah-FEE-ahs)

I like to go to museums and learn about art and history.
Eu gosto de ir a museus e aprender sobre arte e história.
(ehu goh-stoh djee eer ah moo-ZAY-oos ee ah-prehn-DEHR SOH-breh AR-teh ee his-TOH-ryah)

I love to cook and experiment with new recipes in the kitchen.
Eu adoro cozinhar e experimentar novas receitas na cozinha.
(ehu ah-DOH-roh koh-zee-NHAR ee ehks-peh-ree-mehn-TAHR NOH-vaiss reh-SEH-ee-tahs nah koh-ZEE-nhah)

My favorite hobby is playing the piano and composing music.
Meu hobby favorito é tocar piano e compor músicas.
(meh-oo HOH-bee fah-voh-REE-too eh TOH-kahr pee-AH-noh ee kohm-POHR MOO-zee-kahs)

I like to go to the beach and swim in the ocean.
Eu gosto de ir à praia e nadar no mar.
(ehu goh-stoh djee eer ah PRAH-ya ee nah-DAHR noh mar)

I enjoy doing outdoor activities like hiking and camping.
Eu gosto de fazer atividades ao ar livre, como caminhadas e acampamentos.
(ehu goh-stoh djee FAH-zer ah-tee-vee-DAH-dees ah-o ah-r lee-vreh, KOH-moh kah-meen-HAH-dahs ee ah-kahm-pah-MEN-tohss)

I like to travel and experience different cultures and cuisines.
Eu gosto de viajar e experimentar diferentes culturas e culinárias.
(ehu goh-stoh djee vee-ah-ZHAR ee ehks-peh-ree-men-TAHR dee-fer-EN-tes kool-TOO-rass ee koo-lee-NAH-ree-ahss)

I enjoy practicing yoga and meditation for relaxation.
Eu gosto de praticar yoga e meditação para relaxar.
*(ehu goh-stoh djee prah-TEE-kahr YOH-gah ee meh-dee-tah-SAW
pah-rah reh-lah-shahr)*

My favorite hobby is horseback riding and taking care of horses.
Meu hobby favorito é cavalgar e cuidar de cavalos.
*(meh-oo HOH-bee fah-voh-REE-too eh kah-vahl-GAHR ee koo-ee-DAR
djee kah-VAH-lohss)*

I like to attend live theater performances and musicals.
Eu gosto de assistir a apresentações de teatro ao vivo e musicais.
*(ehu goh-stoh djee ah-see-STEE-her ah ah-preh-sen-tah-SOWNS djee
TEH-ah-troh ah-o VEE-voh ee moo-SEE-kah-eece)*

I love to watch and play sports.
Eu adoro assistir e jogar esportes.
(ehu ah-DOH-roh ah-see-STEE-her ee joh-GAHR ess-POR-tess)

MAKING PLANS

What are you up to this weekend?
O que você vai fazer neste fim de semana?
(oh keh voh seh VAH fah-zehr NEST-ee fee-um deh se-mah-nah)

Let's make plans for Saturday.
Vamos fazer planos para sábado.
(VAH-mohs fah-ZEHR PLAH-nohs PAH-rah SAH-bah-doh)

How about we grab dinner on Friday?
Que tal jantarmos juntos na sexta-feira?
(keh TAH-oo zhahn-TAHR-moosh JOON-toosh nah SEHSH-tah-FEH-rah)

Are you free on Saturday afternoon?
Você está livre na tarde de sábado?
(vo-SEH eh-STAH LEE-vreh nah TAHR-deh deh SAH-bah-doh)

Let's get together sometime this week.
Vamos nos encontrar esta semana.
(VAH-mohs nohs ehn-kohn-TRAHR EH-stah SEH-mah-nah)

What's your availability like next week?
Qual é a sua disponibilidade para a próxima semana?
(kwahl eh ah SOO-ah doh-see-vee-lee-dah-DEH PAH-rah ah NOH-shah SEH-mah-nah)

Can we schedule a time to meet up?
Podemos agendar um horário para nos encontrarmos?
(poh-DEH-mohs ah-jehn-DAHR oong oh-RAH-ree-oh PAH-rah nohs ehn-kohn-TRAHR-moosh)

Let's plan something fun for next weekend.
Vamos planejar algo divertido para o próximo fim de semana.
(VAH-mohs plah-neh-JAHR AHL-goh dee-ver-TEE-doh PAH-rah oh PROH-shee-moh fee-um deh se-mah-nah)

How about we go for a hike on Sunday?
Que tal fazermos uma caminhada no domingo?
(keh TAH-oo fah-ZEHR-moosh OO-mah kah-meen-YAH-dah noh doh-MEEN-goh)

Let's plan a road trip for next month.
Vamos planejar uma viagem de carro para o próximo mês.
(VAH-mohs plah-neh-JAHR OO-mah vee-AH-jehm deh KAH-roo PAH-rah oh PROH-kshee-moh MEHSH)

Would you like to join us for drinks tonight?
Você gostaria de nos acompanhar para beber hoje à noite?
(vo-SEH goh-stah-REE-ah deh nohs ah-kohm-pahn-YAHRR PAH-rah beh-BEHR OH-jee ah NOH-ee-tee)

Let's catch up over coffee this week.
Vamos nos encontrar para tomar um café esta semana.
(VAH-mohs nohs ehn-kohn-TRAHR PAH-rah toh-MAHR oong kah-FEH EH-stah SEH-mah-nah)

What's your schedule like for next weekend?
Como está sua agenda para o próximo fim de semana?
(KOH-moh eh-STAH SOO-ah ah-JEHN-dah PAH-rah oh PROH-shee-moh fee-um deh se-mah-nah)

Let's make a reservation for Friday night.
Vamos fazer uma reserva para sexta à noite.
(VAH-mohs fah-ZEHR OO-mah reh-ZEH-vah PAH-rah SEHSH-tah ah NOH-ee-tee)

How about we plan a picnic for Sunday?
Que tal planejarmos um piquenique para o domingo?
(keh TAH-oo plah-neh-JAHR-moosh oong pee-keh-NEE-kee PAH-rah oh doh-MEEN-goh)

Let's organize a movie night this weekend.
Vamos organizar uma noite de cinema neste fim de semana.
(VAH-mohs ohr-gah-nee-ZAH oong-ah NOH-ee-tee deh see-NEH-mah NEHS-tee fee-um deh se-mah-nah)

Would you like to come to a party on Saturday?
Você gostaria de vir para uma festa no sábado?
(vo-SEH goh-stah-REE-ah deh VEER PAH-rah OO-mah FEH-stah noh SAH-bah-doh)

Let's plan a day trip for next weekend.
Vamos planejar um passeio de um dia para o próximo fim de semana.
(VAH-mohs plah-neh-JAHR oong pah-SEH-oo deh oong DEE-ah PAH-rah oh PROH-shee-moh fee-um deh se-mah-nah)

Can we schedule a lunch date next week?
Podemos agendar um encontro para almoçarmos na próxima semana?
(poh-DEH-mohs ah-jehn-DAHR oong ehn-KOHN-troo PAH-rah ahl-moh-SHAHR-moosh nah NOH-shah SEH-mah-nah)

Let's make reservations for brunch on Sunday.
Vamos fazer reservas para um brunch no domingo.
(VAH-mohs fah-ZEHR reh-ZEH-vahs PAH-rah oong BRANSH noh doh-MEEN-goh)

How about we go to a concert next month?
Que tal irmos a um concerto no próximo mês?
(keh TAH-oo eer-moosh ah oong kohn-SEHR-toh noh PROH-kshee-moh MEHSH)

Let's plan a weekend getaway soon.
Vamos planejar uma escapada de fim de semana em breve.
(VAH-mohs plah-neh-JAHR OO-mah ess-kah-PAH-dah deh fee-um deh se-mah-nah ehn BREH-veh)

What do you think about meeting up for dinner tonight?
O que você acha de nos encontrarmos para jantar esta noite?
(oh keh vo-SEH AH-shah deh nohs ehn-kohn-TRAHR-moosh PAH-rah zhahn-TAHR EH-stah NOY-tee)

Let's schedule a meeting for next week.
Vamos agendar uma reunião para a próxima semana.
(VAH-mohs ah-jehn-DAHR OO-mah reh-oo-nee-AW PAH-rah oh PROH-shee-moh SEH-mah-nah)

How about we take a cooking class together?
Que tal fazermos uma aula de culinária juntos?
(keh TAH-oo fah-ZEHR-moosh OO-mah OW-lah deh
koo-lee-NAH-ree-ah JOON-toosh)

Let's plan a beach day for next weekend.
Vamos planejar um dia de praia para o próximo fim de semana.
(VAH-mohs plah-neh-JAHR oong DEE-ah deh PRAH-yah PAH-rah oh
PROH-shee-moh fee-um deh se-mah-nah)

Would you like to go hiking with me next Saturday?
Você gostaria de ir fazer uma caminhada comigo no próximo sábado?
(vo-SEH goh-stah-REE-ah deh eer fah-ZEHR OO-mah kah-mee-NAH-dah
KOH-mee-goh noh PROH-kshee-moh SAH-bah-doh)

Let's make plans to go to the amusement park next month.
Vamos planejar para irmos ao parque de diversões no próximo mês.
(VAH-mohs plah-neh-JAHR PAH-rah eer-moosh ah-oo PAHR-kee jee
dee-vehr-SOHNS noh PROH-kshee-moh MEHSH)

How about we have a game night this Friday?
Que tal termos uma noite de jogos nesta sexta-feira?
(keh TAH-oo TEHR-moosh OO-mah NOH-ee-tee deh JOH-gohs
NEHS-tah SEHSH-tah-FAY-rah)

Let's plan a road trip for next month.
Vamos planejar uma viagem de carro para o próximo mês.
(VAH-mohs plah-neh-JAHR OO-mah VYAH-jehm deh KAH-roh PAH-rah
oh PROH-shee-moh MEHSH)

TALKING ABOUT DAILY ROUTINES

I take a shower in the morning.
Eu tomo banho de manhã.
(Eh-oo TOH-moo BAH-nyoo djee mah-NYAH)

I brush my teeth after breakfast.
Eu escovo os dentes depois do café da manhã.
(Eh-oo ess-KOH-voo oos DJEN-tes DJEH-pwesh doh KAH-fee dah mah-NYAH)

I pack my lunch before leaving for work/school.
Eu preparo meu almoço antes de sair para o trabalho/escola.
(Eh-oo preh-pah-roh meh-oo ahl-MOH-soo BEHN-tchee djee sah-EER pah-rah o tra-BAH-lyoo / ess-KOH-lah)

I commute to work/school.
Eu vou para o trabalho/escola.
(Eh-oo voh pah-rah o tra-BAH-lyoo / ess-KOH-lah)

I arrive at work/school.
Eu chego ao trabalho/escola.
(Eh-oo CHEH-goh ah-oh tra-BAH-lyoo / ess-KOH-lah)

I take a walk during my lunch break.
Eu dou uma caminhada durante a minha pausa para o almoço.
(Eh-oo doh-oo OO-mah kah-MEEN-yah-dah doo-RAN-teh ah meh-oo-nah POW-sah pah-rah oh ahl-MOH-soo)

I continue working/studying in the afternoon.
Eu continuo trabalhando/estudando à tarde.
(Eh-oo kohn-too-EE-noo trah-bah-LYAN-doo / ess-too-DYAN-doo ah TAH-djee)

I have a snack in the afternoon.
Eu faço um lanche à tarde.
(Eh-oo FAH-soo oom LAHN-chee ah TAH-djee)

I commute back home.
Eu volto para casa.
(Eh-oo VOHL-toh pah-rah KAH-sah)

I arrive home.
Eu chego em casa.
(Eh-oo CHEH-goh ehm KAH-sah)

I make dinner.
Eu preparo o jantar.
(Eh-oo preh-pah-roh oh ZHAN-tahr)

I eat dinner.
Eu janto.
(Eh-oo JAHN-too)

I watch TV in the evening.
Eu assisto TV à noite.
(Eh-oo ah-SEES-toh TV ah NOY-tchee)

I read a book in the evening.
Eu leio um livro à noite.
(Eh-oo LEH-yoo oom LEE-vroh ah NOY-tchee)

I take a bath or shower before bed.
Eu tomo banho ou chuveiro antes de dormir.
(Eh-oo TOH-moo BAH-nyoo oh shoo-VAY-roh AHN-tes djee dohr-MEER)

I brush my teeth before bed.
Eu escovo os dentes antes de dormir.
(Eh-oo ess-KOH-voo oos DJEN-tes AHN-tes djee dohr-MEER)

I go to bed at...
Eu vou para a cama às...
(Eh-oo voh pah-rah ah KAH-mah ahsh...)

I fall asleep quickly.
Eu durmo rapidamente.
(Eh-oo DOOR-moh rah-pee-dah-MEN-tee)

I sleep through the night.
Eu durmo a noite toda.
(Eh-oo DOOR-moh ah NOY-tee TOH-dah)

I wake up in the middle of the night.
Eu acordo no meio da noite.
(Eh-oo ah-KOOR-doo noh MAY-oo dah NOY-tchee)

I have trouble falling back to sleep.
Eu tenho dificuldade em voltar a dormir.
(Eh-oo TEH-nyoo dee-fee-kool-DAH-deh ehm vohl-TAHR ah dohr-MEER)

I use an alarm clock to wake up.
Eu uso um despertador para acordar.
(Eh-oo OO-soh oom deh-spehr-tah-DOHR pah-rah ah-kohr-DAHR)

GIVING AND ASKING FOR ADVICE

In my opinion, you should...
Em minha opinião, você deveria...
(ehm MEE-nya oh-pinyow, VOH-seh deh-veh-ree-ah)

From my experience, I would recommend that you...
Com base na minha experiência, eu recomendaria que você...
(kohm BA-see nah MEE-nya ehk-speh-ryen-SEE-ah, EH-oo reh-koh-mehn-DA-ree-ah keh VOH-seh)

If I were in your shoes, I would...
Se eu estivesse no seu lugar, eu...
(seh EH-oo esh-teh-VEH-seh noh seh-oo plah-SEH, EH-oo)

One possible solution could be...
Uma possível solução poderia ser...
(OO-mah PO-see-vehl soh-loo-SOW poh-deh-REE-ah seh)

I think it would be a good idea to...
Eu acho que seria uma boa ideia...
(EH-oo AH-sho keh seh-REE-ah OO-mah BOH-ah ee-DEH-yah)

Why don't you try...
Por que você não tenta...
(pohr keh VOH-seh noh TEHN-tah)

It might be helpful to...
Pode ser útil...
(POH-deh seh ooh-TEEL)

What do you think I should do?
O que você acha que eu deveria fazer?
(OH keh voh-SAY AH-shah keh eh-oo DEH-veh-ree-ah FAH-zehr?)

Can you give me some advice on this?
Você pode me dar algum conselho sobre isso?
(voh-SAY poh-dee meh DAHR ahl-GOOM kohn-SEH-lyoh SOH-breh EE-soh?)

I'm not sure what to do, can you help me out?
Eu não tenho certeza do que fazer, você pode me ajudar?
(EH-oo não TEH-nyoh sehr-TEH-zah doo keh FAH-zehr, voh-SAY poh-deh meh ah-zoo-DAR?)

Do you have any suggestions for me?
Você tem alguma sugestão para mim?
(voh-SAY teh-oo AHL-goo-mah soo-jes-TAO pah-rah meem?)

What would you do in my situation?
O que você faria na minha situação?
(OH keh voh-SAY fah-REE-ah nah MEENH-ah see-too-AH-saw?)

Could you give me your opinion on this matter?
Você poderia me dar sua opinião sobre este assunto?
(voh-SAY poh-deh-REE-ah meh DAHR SOO-ah oh-pee-nee-YAO SOH-breh EH-steh ah-SOON-toh?)

I'm looking for some guidance, any thoughts?
Estou procurando por algum direcionamento, tem alguma ideia?
(ess-TOH proh-koo-RAHN-doh por AHL-goom dee-reh-see-oh-nah-MEN-toh, teh-oo AHL-goom-ah ee-DEH-yah?)

What's your take on this?
Qual é a sua opinião sobre isso?
(kwahl eh ah SOO-ah oh-pee-nee-YAO SOH-breh EE-soh?)

Can you offer any insights on this issue?
Você pode oferecer algum insight sobre este problema?
(voh-SAY poh-deh oh-feh-REH-sehr AHL-goom een-SAIHT SOH-breh EH-steh proh-BLEH-mah?)

144

I'd appreciate your input on this.
Eu apreciaria sua contribuição sobre isso.
(EH-oo ah-preh-see-AH-ree-ah SOO-ah kon-tree-boo-ee-SAW SOH-breh EE-soh.)

Do you have any recommendations?
Você tem alguma recomendação?
(voh-SAY teh-oo AHL-goom-ah reh-koh-mehn-dah-SAW?)

I need some advice, can you give me some direction?
Eu preciso de um conselho, você pode me dar alguma direção?
(EH-oo preh-SEE-zoh jee oong kohn-SEH-lyoh, voh-SAY poh-deh meh DAHR AHL-goom-ah dee-reh-SEE-oh?)

What's your advice on how to handle this?
Qual é o seu conselho sobre como lidar com isso?
(kwahl eh oh SEH-oo kohn-SEH-lyoh SOH-breh KOH-moh lee-DAHR kohm EE-soh?)

Can you share any wisdom on this topic?
Você pode compartilhar alguma sabedoria sobre este assunto?
(voh-SAY poh-deh kohn-pahr-tee-LHAR AHL-goom-ah sah-beh-DOH-ree-ah SOH-breh EH-steh ah-SOON-toh?)

I'm seeking some guidance, can you point me in the right direction?
Estou buscando alguma orientação, você pode me apontar na direção certa?
(ess-TOH BOO-skahn-doh AHL-goom-ah oh-ree-en-tah-see-oh, voh-SAY poh-deh meh ah-PON-tahr nah dee-reh-SEE-oh SEHR-tah?)

TALKING ABOUT LIKES AND DISLIKES

I really like it.
Eu realmente gosto disso.
(eh-oo reh-al-MEN-te gos-TOH DEES-soh)

I'm a big fan of it.
Eu sou um grande fã disso.
(eh-oo soh oom GRAHN-deh fahn DEES-soh)

I'm fond of it.
Eu gosto disso.
(eh-oo GOS-toh DEES-soh)

It's one of my favorites.
É um dos meus favoritos.
(EH oong doos MEH-oosh fa-voh-REE-toosh)

I enjoy it.
Eu aprecio isso.
(eh-oo ah-pree-SEE-oh DEES-soh)

It's right up my alley.
É exatamente o meu tipo.
(EH eh-zahk-ta-MEN-teh oh may-oo TEE-po)

It's right up my street.
É bem do meu agrado.
(EH beeng doo may-oo ah-GRA-dooh)

I'm really into it.
Eu realmente curto isso.
(eh-oo reh-al-MEN-teh KOOR-tooh DEES-soh)

I'm crazy about it.
Eu sou louco*(a)* por isso.
(eh-oo soh LOH-koo(pohr) EE-soh)

I can't get enough of it.
Eu não consigo ter o suficiente disso.
(eh-oo NAH-o kohn-SEE-goh tehr oh soo-fee-SEE-ehn-tee DEES-soh)

It's my cup of tea.
É a minha praia.
(EH ah MEE-nha PRAI-ya)

It's my jam.
É a minha praia.
(EH ah MEE-nha PRAI-ya)

It's my thing.
É a minha praia.
(EH ah MEE-nha PRAI-ya)

I have a soft spot for it.
Tenho um carinho especial por isso.
(TEHN-yoo oong kah-REE-nyoo es-peh-SYAL pohr DEES-soh)

It's my go-to.
É o meu favorito.
(EH oh may-oo fah-voh-REE-tooh)

I don't like it.
Eu não gosto disso.
(eh-oo nao GOH-stoh DEE-soh)

It's not my cup of tea.
Não é a minha praia.
(nah-ooh EH ah MEE-nha PRAH-ee-ah)

I can't stand it.
Não suporto isso.
(nah-ooh soo-POHR-toh EE-soh)

It's not for me.
Não é para mim.
(nah-ooh EH PAH-rah meen)

I have a strong aversion to it.
Tenho uma forte aversão por isso.
(TEN-yoh OO-mah FORTCH-ee ah-vair-SAWNG pohr EE-soh)

I'm not a fan of it.
Não sou fã disso.
(nah-ooh sow FAH DEE-soh)

I'm not keen on it.
Não estou interessado nisso.
(nah-ooh eh-STOH-oo een-tche-ress-AH-doh NEES-soh)

It doesn't appeal to me.
Não me atrai.
(nah-ooh mee ah-TRAY)

It's not my thing.
Não é a minha praia.
(nah-ooh EH ah MEE-nha PRAH-ee-ah)

I'm not fond of it.
Não sou fã disso.
(nah-ooh sow FAH DEE-soh)

It leaves a bad taste in my mouth.
Deixa um gosto ruim na minha boca.
(DAY-shah oong GOH-stoh HOO-eeng nah MEE-nha BOH-kah)

It's a turn-off for me.
Isso me desanima.
(EE-soh mee day-sah-NEE-mah)

I find it unpleasant.
Acho isso desagradável.
(AH-shoh EE-soh day-sah-grah-DAH-vehl)

It bothers me.
Isso me incomoda.
(EE-soh mee een-koh-MOH-dah)

It rubs me the wrong way.
Isso me irrita.
(EE-soh mee ee-ree-TAH)

EXPRESSING AGREEMENT OR DISAGREEMENT

I completely agree.
Eu concordo completamente.
(eyoo kohn-kohr-doh kohm-pleh-tah-mehn-tee.)

That's a great point.
Isso é um ótimo ponto.
(eeso eh oom OH-tee-moh POHN-too.)

I couldn't agree more.
Não poderia concordar mais.
(nah-oo poh-deh-ree-ah kohn-kohr-DAHR mah-ees.)

You're absolutely right.
Você está absolutamente correto.
(voh-seh eh-STAH ahb-soo-loo-tah-MEHN-tee ko-RREH-ktoo.)

I see what you mean.
Eu entendo o que você quer dizer.
(eyoo ehn-TEHN-doh ooh keh voh-seh kehreh dee-ZEHR.)

That's exactly my thinking.
Isso é exatamente o que eu estava pensando.
(eeso eh eh-zahk-tah-MEHN-tee mahy TEEN-kee-ng.)

That's a valid point.
Esse é um ponto válido.
(EH-sih eh oom POHN-too VAH-lee-doh.)

I'm on the same page.
Estamos na mesma página.
(ehs-TOH-mohs nah MEH-sma PAY-jee-nah.)

I concur with you.
Eu concordo com você.
(eyoo kohn-KOHR-doh kohm voh-SEH.)

That's precisely what I was thinking.
Isso é exatamente o que eu estava pensando.
(eeso eh eh-zahk-tah-MEHN-tee oh keh eyoo ehs-TAH-va pehn-SAHN-doo.)

I respectfully disagree.
Eu discordo respeitosamente.
(eyoo dee-KOHR-doh rehs-pey-TOO-zah-men-teh.)

I'm afraid I don't agree.
Receio que eu não concorde.
(reh-SEH-oh keh eyoo nah-oo kohn-KOHR-deh.)

I'm not so sure about that.
Não estou tão certo sobre isso.
(nah-oo eh-STOH tahn SEHR-toh soh-breh eeso.)

I have a different perspective.
Eu tenho uma perspectiva diferente.
(eyoo TEH-nyoo oo-mah pehr-spehk-TEE-vah dee-feh-REHN-teh.)

That's not quite how I see it.
Não é exatamente como eu vejo.
(nah-oo eh eh-zahk-tah-MEHN-tee koh-moo eyoo VEY-joh.)

I'm of a different opinion.
Tenho uma opinião diferente.
(TEH-nyoo oo-mah oh-pee-nyahw dee-feh-REHN-teh.)

I'm not convinced.
Não estou convencido.
(nah-oo eh-STOH kohn-vehn-SEE-doh.)

I beg to differ.
Eu discordo.
(eyoo behg too dee-FEHR.)

I'm not entirely in agreement.
Não concordo totalmente.
(nah-oo kohn-KOHR-doh toh-tahl-men-tee.)

That's not my understanding.
Não é como eu entendo.
(nah-oo eh koh-moo eyoo ehn-tehn-doh.)

I see things differently.
Eu vejo as coisas de forma diferente.
(eyoo VEH-joh ahs KOY-zahs deh FOHR-mah dee-feh-REHN-teh.)

That's not necessarily true.
Isso não é necessariamente verdade.
(eeso nah-oo eh neh-seh-sah-REE-ah-men-tee VEH-ryahdjee.)

I don't think that's accurate.
Eu não acho que isso seja preciso.
(eyoo nah-oo AH-shoh keh eeso SEH-jah preh-SEE-zoo.)

I have a different take on this.
Tenho uma visão diferente sobre isso.
(TEH-nyoo oo-mah vee-ZAHW dee-feh-REHN-teh soh-breh eeso.)

I'm sorry, but I can't agree with you on this.
Sinto muito, mas não posso concordar com você sobre isso.
(SEEN-toh MOOR-toh, mahs nah-oo POH-soh kohn-KOHR-dahr kohm voh-SEH soh-breh eeso.)

You've hit the nail on the head.
Você acertou em cheio.
(voh-SEH ah-seh-TOO-oo ehn CHEY-oo.)

I totally agree with you.
Eu concordo totalmente com você.
(eyoo kohn-KOHR-doh toh-tahl-men-tee kohm voh-SEH.)

I share your opinion.

Eu compartilho sua opinião.

(eyoo kohm-pahr-TEE-lyoh soo-ah oh-pee-nee-AW.)

I'm in full agreement.

Estou em pleno acordo.

(eh-stoh ehm PLEH-noo ah-KWOHR-doo.)

That's spot on.

Isso está perfeito.

(EE-soh EH-stah peh-REH-ftoo.)

MAKING EXCUSES

I'm sorry, but I have a prior commitment.
Lo sinto, mas eu tenho um compromisso anterior.
(loh SEEN-too, mahz eh-yoo TEHN-yoo oong kohm-pruh-MEE-soo ahn-tee-OHR)

Unfortunately, I won't be able to make it.
Infelizmente, eu não poderei comparecer.
(een-fay-LEEZ-mehn-tee, eh-yoo noun poh-deh-RAY kohm-pah-REH-sair)

I'm really sorry, but I have to attend to something else.
Eu sinto muito, mas eu tenho que atender a outra coisa.
(eh-yoo SEEN-too MOO-too, mahs eh-yoo TEHN-yoo kee ah-ten-DEHR ah oh-TRA ko-ee-zah)

I apologize, but I won't be able to attend.
Eu peço desculpas, mas eu não poderei comparecer.
(eh-yoo PEH-soh dess-KOOL-pahs, mahs eh-yoo noun poh-deh-RAY kohm-pah-REH-sair)

I'm afraid I can't come due to personal reasons.
Temo que não possa vir por motivos pessoais.
(TEH-moh keh noun POH-sah veer pohr moh-TEE-vohs peh-SOH-aysh)

Regrettably, I won't be able to make it.
Infelizmente, não poderei comparecer.
(een-fay-LEEZ-mehn-tee, noun poh-deh-RAY kohm-pah-REH-sair)

I'm sorry, but something urgent came up.
Lo sinto, mas algo urgente surgiu.
(loh SEEN-too, mahs AHL-goh oor-JEHN-tee SOOR-joo)

I apologize, but I won't be able to attend.
Eu peço desculpas, mas não poderei comparecer.
(eh-yoo PEH-soh dess-KOOL-pahs, mahs noun poh-deh-RAY kohm-pah-REH-sair)

I'm afraid I have to decline due to unforeseen circumstances.
Tenho que declinar devido a circunstâncias imprevistas.
(TEHN-yoo keh day-klee-NAHR deh-VEE-doh ah seer-koon-stahn-see-AHS een-preh-VEES-tahs)

I'm sorry, but I have a family emergency to attend to.
Lo sinto, mas tenho uma emergência familiar para atender.
(loh SEEN-too, mahs TEHN-yoo OO-mah eh-mehr-JEN-see-ah fah-mee-LEE-yahr pah-rah ah-ten-DEHR)

Unfortunately, I won't be able to make it due to transportation issues.
Infelizmente, não poderei comparecer devido a problemas de transporte.
(een-fay-LEEZ-mehn-tee, noun poh-deh-RAY kohm-pah-REH-sair deh-VEE-doh ah proh-BLEH-mahs jee trahn-SPOHR-tee)

I'm sorry, but I have a prior engagement that I can't miss.
Lo sinto, mas tenho um compromisso anterior que não posso perder.
(loh SEEN-too, mahs TEHN-yoo oong kohm-pree-MEE-soo ahn-tee-OHR keh noun POH-soh PEHR-dehr)

I'm afraid I can't come due to health reasons.
Tenho receio de não poder vir devido a motivos de saúde.
(TEHN-yoo reh-SAY-oh jee noun poh-DEHR veer deh-VEE-doh ah moh-TEE-vohs jee sah-OH-deh)

I wish I could, but I have a deadline to meet.
Gostaria de poder, mas tenho um prazo a cumprir.
(gohs-TAH-ree-ah jee POH-dehr, mahs TEHN-yoo oong PRAH-zoo ah KOOM-pree-rr)

I'm sorry, but I won't be able to attend because of a work obligation.
Lo sinto, mas não poderei comparecer devido a uma obrigação de trabalho.
(loh SEEN-too, mahs noun poh-deh-RAY kohm-pah-REH-sair deh-VEE-doh ah OO-mah oh-bree-gah-SOWN jee trah-BAH-lyoo)

I apologize, but I have to take care of something important.
Eu peço desculpas, mas tenho que cuidar de algo importante.
(eh-yoo PEH-soh dess-KOOL-pahs, mahs TEHN-yoo keh koo-ee-DAHR jee AHL-goh een-pohr-TAHN-teh)

I'm afraid I won't be able to make it because of financial constraints.
Tenho receio de não poder vir devido a restrições financeiras.
(TEHN-yoo reh-SAY-oh jee noun poh-DEHR veer deh-VEE-doh ah rehs-tree-SEWNSS fih-nahn-SEH-rahss)

I'm sorry, but I have a conflicting commitment that day.
Lo sinto, mas tenho um compromisso que conflita com esse dia.
(loh SEEN-too, mahs TEHN-yoo oong kohm-pree-MEE-soo keh kohn-FLEE-tah kohm EH-see DEE-ah)

I'm sorry, but I'm not feeling well and won't be able to attend.
Lo sinto, mas não estou me sentindo bem e não poderei comparecer.
(loh SEEN-too, mahs noun EH-stoh meh sen-TEEN-doh beeng ee noun poh-deh-RAY kohm-pah-REH-sair)

I'm sorry, but I already made other plans for that day.
Lo sinto, mas já fiz outros planos para esse dia.
(loh SEEN-too, mahs jah feez OHN-troos PLAH-noos pah-rah EH-see DEE-ah)

I'm afraid I won't be able to come because of personal reasons.
Tenho receio de não poder vir devido a motivos pessoais.
(TEHN-yoo reh-SAY-oh jee noun poh-DEHR veer deh-VEE-doh ah moh-TEE-vohs peh-SOY-ays)

I'm sorry, but I have a doctor's appointment that day.
Lo sinto, mas tenho uma consulta médica nesse dia.
(loh SEEN-too, mahs TEHN-yoo OO-mah kohn-SOOL-tah MEH-dee-kah NEH-see DEE-ah)

I apologize, but I have unexpected circumstances to deal with.
Peço desculpas, mas tenho circunstâncias inesperadas para lidar.
(PEH-soh dess-KOOL-pahs, mahs TEHN-yoo seer-koon-stahn-see-AHS een-eh-speh-RAH-dahs pah-rah lee-DAHR)

I'm afraid I won't be able to attend due to a personal emergency.
Tenho receio de não poder comparecer devido a uma emergência pessoal.
(TEHN-yoo reh-SAY-oh jee noun poh-DEHR kohm-pah-REH-sair deh-VEE-doh ah OO-mah eh-mehr-JEN-see-ah peh-SOY-ahl)

I'm sorry, but I have a prior engagement that I can't cancel.
Lo sinto, mas tenho um compromisso anterior que não posso cancelar.
(loh SEEN-too, mahs TEHN-yoo oong kohm-pree-MEE-soo ahn-teh-YOHR kee noun POH-soo kahn-sah-LAHR)

I'm sorry, but I have to take care of my pet that day.
Lo sinto, mas tenho que cuidar do meu animal de estimação nesse dia.
(loh SEEN-too, mahs TEHN-yoo keh koo-ee-DAHR doh MEH-ooh ah-nee-MOWL deh eh-stee-mah-SAWN NEH-see DEE-ah)

I'm afraid I can't attend due to transportation issues.
Tenho receio de não poder comparecer devido a problemas de transporte.
(TEHN-yoo reh-SAY-oh jee noun poh-DEHR kohm-pah-REH-sair deh-VEE-doh ah proh-BLEH-mahss deh trahn-spor-teh)

I'm sorry, but I have a work obligation that day.
Lo sinto, mas tenho uma obrigação de trabalho nesse dia.
(loh SEEN-too, mahs TEHN-yoo OO-mah oh-bree-gah-SAWN dee trah-BAH-lyoo NEH-see DEE-ah)

I apologize, but I simply can't make it that day.
Peço desculpas, mas simplesmente não posso ir nesse dia.
(PEH-soh dess-KOOL-pahs, mahs seem-PLYS-mehn-tee noun POH-soo eer NEH-see DEE-ah)

ASKING AND GIVING PERMISSION

Can I borrow your pen, please?
Posso emprestar sua caneta, por favor?
(PO-so em-presh-TAR SU-a ca-NE-ta, por fa-VOR)

May I use the restroom?
Posso usar o banheiro?
(PO-so u-ZAR o ba-NHEI-ro)

Could I leave work a bit early today?
Posso sair um pouco mais cedo hoje?
(PO-so SA-ir um PO-co mais CE-do HO-je)

Would it be okay if I took a day off next week?
Estaria tudo bem se eu tirasse um dia de folga na próxima semana?
(es-ta-RI-a TU-do BEM se eu ti-RAS-se um DIA de FOL-ga na PRÓ-xi-ma SE-ma-na)

Is it alright if I take a photo of this painting?
Posso tirar uma foto desta pintura?
(PO-so ti-RAR u-ma FO-to DES-ta pin-TU-ra)

Can I speak with your supervisor, please?
Posso falar com o seu supervisor, por favor?
(PO-so fa-LAR com o seu su-per-VI-sor, por fa-VOR)

May I have your permission to share this information?
Posso ter a sua permissão para compartilhar esta informação?
(PO-so TER a SU-a per-miS-são pa-ra com-par-TI-lhar ES-ta in-for-ma-ção)

Would it be possible for me to borrow your car?
Seria possível me emprestar o seu carro?
(se-RI-a pos-SÍ-vel me em-PRES-tar o seu CA-rro)

Do you mind if I turn on the air conditioning?
Você se importa se eu ligar o ar-condicionado?
(VO-cê se im-POR-ta se eu li-GAR o ar-con-di-ci-o-NA-do)

Is it okay if I invite a friend to dinner tonight?
Tudo bem se eu convidar um amigo para jantar hoje à noite?
(TU-do BEM se eu con-VI-dar um a-MI-go pa-ra JAN-tar HO-je à NOI-te)

Can I use your phone for a quick call?
Posso usar o seu telefone para uma ligação rápida?
(PO-so u-ZAR o seu te-LE-fo-ne pa-ra u-ma li-ga-ÇÃO RÁ-pi-da)

Would you allow me to bring my dog inside?
Você permitiria que eu trouxesse meu cachorro para dentro?
(VO-cê per-mi-TI-ria que eu trou-XES-se meu ca-CHO-rrro pa-ra DEN-tro)

May I have your permission to use this photograph in my presentation?
Posso ter a sua permissão para usar esta fotografia na minha apresentação?
(PO-so TER a SU-a per-miS-são pa-ra u-SAR ES-ta fo-to-GRA-fia na MI-nha a-pre-sen-ta-ÇÃO)

Can I leave my coat here while I run errands?
Posso deixar meu casaco aqui enquanto eu faço recados?
(PO-so dei-XAR meu ca-SA-co A-qui en-QUAN-to eu FA-ço re-CA-dos?)

Would it be alright if I parked my car in your driveway?
Estaria tudo bem se eu estacionasse o meu carro na sua garagem?
(es-ta-RI-a TU-do BEM se eu es-ta-ci-o-NAS-se o meu CA-rro na SU-a ga-RA-gem?)

Sure, you can borrow my pen.
Claro, você pode emprestar minha caneta.
(CLA-ro, VO-cê PO-de em-presh-TAR MI-nha ca-NE-ta)

Of course, you may use the restroom.
Claro, você pode usar o banheiro.
(CLA-ro, VO-cê PO-de u-ZAR o ba-NHEI-ro)

Yes, you can leave work a bit early today.
Sim, você pode sair um pouco mais cedo hoje.
(SIM, VO-cê PO-de SA-ir um PO-co mais CE-do HO-je)

Yes, it's okay for you to take a day off next week.
Sim, está tudo bem se você tirar um dia de folga na próxima semana.
(SIM, es-TÁ TU-do BEM se VO-cê ti-RAR u-m DI-a de FOL-ga na PRÓ-xi-ma SE-ma-na)

Absolutely, you can take a photo of this painting.
Absolutamente, você pode tirar uma foto desta pintura.
(AB-so-LU-ta-MEN-te, VO-cê PO-de ti-RAR u-ma FO-to DES-ta pin-TU-ra)

Yes, you can speak with my supervisor.
Sim, você pode falar com o meu supervisor.
(SIM, VO-cê PO-de fa-LAR com o MEU su-per-VI-sor)

Certainly, you have my permission to share this information.
Certamente, você tem a minha permissão para compartilhar esta informação.
(cer-TA-men-te, VO-cê tem a MI-nha per-miS-são pa-ra com-par-TI-lhar ES-ta in-for-ma-ção)

Yes, it's possible for you to borrow my car.
Sim, é possível você emprestar o meu carro.
(SIM, é pos-SÍ-vel VO-cê em-PRES-tar o MEU CA-rro)

No problem, go ahead and turn on the air conditioning.
Sem problema, pode ligar o ar condicionado.
(sehm proh-BLEH-mah, POH-deh lee-GAHR oh ahr kohn-dee-see-oh-NAH-doh.)

Yes, you can invite your friend to dinner tonight.
Sim, pode convidar seu amigo para jantar hoje à noite.
(seem, POH-dee kohn-vee-DAHR seh-oo ah-MEE-goh pah-rah JAHN-tahr OH-je ah NOY-tchee.)

Sure, you can use my phone for a quick call.
Claro, pode usar meu telefone para uma ligação rápida.
(KLAH-roh, POH-deh oo-ZAHR meh-oo teh-leh-FOH-neh pah-rah OO-mah lee-gah-SOW ra-PEE-dah.)

Yes, I'll allow you to bring your dog inside.
Sim, vou permitir que traga seu cachorro para dentro.
(seem, voh pehr-MEE-teer keh TRAH-gah seh-oo kah-SHOH-roo pah-rah DEN-troo.)

Yes, you have my permission to use this photograph in your presentation.
Sim, tem minha permissão para usar esta fotografia em sua apresentação.
(seem, teh-oo mee-nya pehr-mee-SOW pah-rah oo-ZAHR EH-stah fo-toh-grah-fee-ah ehm soo-ah ah-preh-sen-tah-SOW.)

Yes, you can leave your coat here while you run errands.
Sim, pode deixar seu casaco aqui enquanto faz seus recados.
(seem, POH-deh dey-SHAHR seh-oo kah-SAH-koh ah-KEE een-kwahn-toh fahz seus reh-KAH-dohs.)

Yes, it's alright for you to park your car in my driveway.
Sim, está tudo bem se estacionar seu carro em minha garagem.
(seem, EH-stah TOO-doh behm seh es-tah-syo-NAHR seh-oo KAH-roo ehm MEE-nyah gah-RAH-jem.)

EXPRESSING GRATITUDE AND APOLOGIES

Thank you so much!
Muito obrigado!
(MOO-ee-toh oh-bree-GAH-doh)

I really appreciate it.
Eu realmente aprecio isso.
(eh-oo reh-ahl-MEHN-tee ah-preh-SEE-oh EE-soh)

You have my heartfelt thanks.
Você tem meu agradecimento sincero.
(voh-SAY tehn meh-oo ah-grah-deh-SEE-men-toh seen-SEH-roo)

I can't thank you enough.
Eu não posso agradecer o suficiente.
(eh-oo nah-ooh POH-soo ah-grah-deh-SEHR oh soo-fee-see-YEHN-tee)

Your kindness means the world to me. -
Sua gentileza significa o mundo para mim.
(SOO-ah jehn-tee-LEH-zah seen-ee-foo-CAH oh MOON-doh PAH-rah meh)

You've been so helpful.
Você tem sido tão útil.
(voh-SAY tehn SEE-dee-oo tah-ooh OO-teel)

I'm grateful for your support.
Sou grato pelo seu apoio.
(soh GRAH-too PEH-loh seh-oo ah-POY-oh)

I'm so lucky to have you.
Sou tão sortudo por ter você.
(soh tah-ooh sohr-TOO-doh pohr TEHR voh-SAY)

I'm deeply grateful for everything you've done.
Sou profundamente grato por tudo o que você fez.
(soh proh-fewn-DAH-mehn-tee GRAH-too pohr TOO-doh oh keh voh-SAY fehz)

Your generosity is truly appreciated.
Sua generosidade é muito apreciada.
(SOO-ah jeh-neh-roh-see-DAH-deh eh MOO-ee-toh ah-preh-see-AH-dah)

Thanks a million!
Muito obrigado!
(MOO-ee-toh oh-bree-GAH-doh)

You're a lifesaver.
Você é um salvador.
(voh-SAY eh oohm sahl-vah-DOHR)

Thank you from the bottom of my heart.
Obrigado do fundo do meu coração.
(oh-bree-GAH-doh doh FOON-doh doh meh-oo koh-rah-SOWN)

You have my sincerest thanks.
Você tem meu agradecimento mais sincero.
(voh-SAY tehn meh-oo ah-grah-deh-SEE-men-toh mah-eez seen-SEH-roo)

I can't express my gratitude enough.
Não consigo expressar minha gratidão o suficiente.
(nah-ooh kohn-SEE-goh ehk-spree-SAHR MEE-nah grah-tee-DAW oh soo-fee-SEE-YEHN-tee)

I'm sorry.
Desculpe-me.
(dess-KOOL-peh meh)

Please forgive me.
Por favor, me perdoe.
(pohr fah-VOHR, meh pehr-DOH-eh)

I apologize.
Eu peço desculpas.
(eh-oo PEH-soh dess-KOOL-pahs)

I'm so sorry for what I've done.
Sinto muito pelo que eu fiz.
(SEEN-too MOO-too PEH-loh keh eh-oo feez)

I'm truly sorry.
Sinto muito mesmo.
(SEEN-too MOO-too MEH-moo)

I take full responsibility for my actions.
Assumo total responsabilidade pelas minhas ações.
(ah-SOO-moo toh-TAHL heh-spoon-sah-beh-LEE-dah-deh PEH-lahs MEE-nhahs AH-soh-ens)

I'm sorry for any inconvenience I may have caused.
Desculpe-me por qualquer inconveniente que eu possa ter causado.
(dess-KOOL-peh meh pohr KWAHL-quer een-kohm-VEH-nee-ehn-tee keh eh-oo POH-sah tehr kahw-ZAH-doh)

Please accept my sincerest apologies.
Por favor, aceite minhas mais sinceras desculpas.
(pohr fah-VOHR, ah-SEY-teh MEE-nhahs mah-eez seen-SEH-rahsh dess-KOOL-pahs)

I'm sorry for my mistake.
Desculpe-me pelo meu erro.
(dess-KOOL-peh meh PEH-loh meh-oo EH-roo)

I regret my actions and am sorry for any harm caused.
Lamento minhas ações e peço desculpas por qualquer dano causado.
(lah-MEN-too MEE-nhahs ah-soh-ens eh PEH-soh dess-KOOL-pahs pohr KWAHL-quer DAH-noh kahw-ZAH-doh)

I apologize for my behavior.
Peço desculpas pelo meu comportamento.
(PEH-soh dess-KOOL-pahs PEH-loh meh-oo kohm-pohr-tah-MEN-too)

I'm sorry for my part in this.

Desculpe-me pela minha parte nisso.

(dess-KOOL-peh meh PEH-lah MEE-nhah PAHR-cheh NEES-soo)

I'm sorry for not thinking things through.

Desculpe-me por não ter pensado direito.

(dess-KOOL-peh meh pohr nah-ooh TEHR pehn-SAH-doh dee-REY-toh)

I'm sorry for my poor judgment.

Peço desculpas por meu julgamento falho.

(PEH-soh dess-KOOL-pahs pohr meh-oo jool-gah-MEN-too FA-lyoo)

I'm sorry for letting you down.

Desculpe-me por decepcionar você.

(dess-KOOL-peh meh pohr dee-seh-pee-oh-NAHR voh-seh)

GIVING AND RECEIVING COMPLIMENTS

You look amazing!
você está incrível!
(voh-SEH es-TAH in-KREE-vel)

You're killing it today!
Você está arrasando hoje!
(voh-SEH es-TAH ah-ha-SAHN-do OH-jee)

That outfit suits you so well!
Essa roupa te cai muito bem!
(EHS-sah ROH-pah teh KAI MOO-choh behn)

Your hair looks great!
Seu cabelo está ótimo!
(SEH-oo kah-BEH-loh es-TAH OH-tee-moh)

You're so talented!
Você é muito talentoso/a!
(voh-SEH eh MOO-choo tal-en-TOH-soh/ah)

You have a great sense of humor!
Você tem um ótimo senso de humor!
(voh-SEH teh-oo oohm OH-tee-moh SEN-soo deh OO-mohr)

You always make me smile!
Você sempre me faz sorrir!
(voh-SEH SEM-preh meh FAHZ soh-REE)

I love your energy!
Eu amo a sua energia!
(EH-oo AH-moh ah SOO-ah en-ehr-JEE-ah)

Your work is incredible!
Seu trabalho é incrível!
(SEH-oo trah-BAH-lyoo eh in-KREE-vehl)

You're such a great listener!
Você é um ótimo ouvinte!
(voh-SEH eh oohm OH-tee-moh oh-VEEN-teh)

You're so thoughtful!
Você é tão atencioso/a!
(voh-SEH eh TAH-ooh ah-tehn-see-OH-soh/ah)

You have a beautiful smile!
Você tem um sorriso lindo!
(voh-SEH teh-oo oohm soh-REE-soh LEEN-doov

Your cooking is delicious!
Sua comida é deliciosa!
(SOO-ah koh-MEE-dah eh deh-lee-SEE-oh-sah)

You have such a great voice!
Você tem uma voz incrível!
(voh-SEH teh-oo OO-mah VOHZ in-KREE-vehl)

Your writing is impressive!
Sua escrita é impressionante!
(SOO-ah es-KREE-tah eh eem-preh-see-oh-NAN-tee)

Thank you so much!
Muito obrigado/a!
(MOO-ee-toh oh-bree-GAH-doh/dah)

That's so kind of you to say!
Isso é muito gentil da sua parte!
(EE-soh eh MOO-ee-toh zhehn-TEEL dah SOO-ah PAHR-chee)

I really appreciate that!
Eu realmente agradeço por isso!
(EH-oo reh-ah-men-tee ah-grah-DEH-soh por EE-soh)

Thank you, you made my day!
Obrigado/a, você alegrarou meu dia!
(oh-bree-GAH-doh/dah, voh-SEH ah-leh-GRAH-roh MEH-oo DEE-ah)

That means a lot to me!
Isso significa muito para mim!
(EE-soh sig-nee-fee-kah MOO-ee-toh PAH-rah meh)

Thank you, I worked hard on it!
Obrigado/a, eu trabalhei duro nisso!
(oh-bree-GAH-doh/dah, EH-oo trah-bah-LAY EE-oo-doh-roo NEE-soh)

I'm flattered, thank you!
Estou lisonjeado/a, obrigado/a!
(eh-STOH lee-sohn-zheh-AH-doh/dah, oh-bree-GAH-doh/dah)

You're too sweet, thank you!
Você é muito doce, obrigado/a!
(voh-SEH eh MOO-choh DOH-see, oh-bree-GAH-doh/dah)

Thank you, that's very thoughtful of you!
Obrigado/a, isso é muito atencioso da sua parte!
(oh-bree-GAH-doh/dah, EE-soh eh MOO-ee-toh ah-tehn-see-OH-soh dah SOO-ah PAHR-chee)

Thank you, I'm glad you like it!
Obrigado/a, fico feliz que você tenha gostado!
(oh-bree-GAH-doh/dah, FEE-koh fuh-LEEZ keh voh-SEH TEH-nah gohs-TAH-doh)

That's really nice of you to say, thank you!
Isso é realmente gentil da sua parte, obrigado/a!
(EE-soh eh reh-ah-men-tee zhehn-TEEL dah SOO-ah PAHR-chee, oh-bree-GAH-doh/dah)

I'm so happy to hear that, thank you!
Fico muito feliz em ouvir isso, obrigado/a!
(FEE-koh MOO-choo fuh-LEEZ ehm oh-VEER EE-soh, oh-bree-GAH-doh/dah)

Thank you, I'm humbled!

Obrigado/a, fico humilde!

(oh-bree-GAH-doh/dah, FEE-koh oom-DEEL)

That's very encouraging, thank you!

Isso é muito encorajador, obrigado/a!

(EE-soh eh MOO-ee-toh ehn-koh-rah-ZHA-dohr, oh-bree-GAH-doh/dah)

Thank you, I'm grateful for your kind words!

Obrigado/a, sou grato/a por suas palavras gentis!

(oh-bree-GAH-doh/dah, sohoo GRAH-too/dah pohr SOO-ahs pah-LAH-vrahs zhehn-TEES)

MAKING PHONE CALLS

May I speak to [Name]?
Posso falar com [Nome]?
(POH-soh fah-LAR kohm [NOH-meh]?)

Could you please connect me to the appropriate department?
Poderia me conectar ao departamento apropriado, por favor?
(poh-deh-REE-ah meh koh-nehk-TAHR ah-oh deh-pahr-tah-MEN-toh ah-proh-pee-AH-doh, por fah-VOHR?)

Can you tell me more about [product/service]?
Você pode me dizer mais sobre [produto/serviço]?
(voh-SAY poh-deh meh dee-ZEHR mah-eez oh-BROH [proh-DOO-toh/sehr-VEE-soh]?)

I'm interested in learning more about your company
Eu tenho interesse em saber mais sobre a sua empresa
(yoo TEH-nyoh een-TEH-reh-see een seh-BEHR mah-eez soh-BREH ah soo-ah em-PREH-zah)

I'd like to schedule an appointment/meeting
Eu gostaria de marcar um compromisso/reunião
(yoo goh-stah-REE-ah deh MAHR-kahr oong kohm-pree-MEE-soh/reh-yoo-NEE-ao)

Is there a convenient time for us to discuss this further?
Existe um horário conveniente para conversarmos sobre isso?
(eh-SHEES-teh oong oh-RAR-ee-oh kohm-veh-NEE-ehn-teh pah-rah kohn-ver-SAR-mohs soo-BREH EE-soh?)

May I leave a message for [Name]?
Posso deixar uma mensagem para [Nome]?
(POH-soh day-SHAHR oong-AH mess-AH-jee pah-rah [NOH-meh]?)

Could you please have [Name] call me back?
Você poderia pedir para que [Nome] me ligue de volta?
*(voh-SAY poh-deh-REE-ah peh-DEER pah-rah keh [NOH-meh] meh
LEE-ghee deh VOHL-tah?)*

Can you provide me with more information on [product/service]?
Você pode me fornecer mais informações sobre [produto/serviço]?
*(voh-SAY poh-deh meh fohr-neh-SAYR mah-eez een-fohr-mah-SOHN-
soh-breh [proh-DOO-toh/sehr-VEE-soh]?)*

I have a complaint regarding [issue].
Eu tenho uma reclamação sobre [questão].
(yoo TEH-nyoh oo-mah reh-klah-mah-SOWN soo-BREH [keh-STAO])

Can you help me resolve this issue with [product/service]?
Você pode me ajudar a resolver este problema com [produto/serviço]?
*(voh-SAY poh-deh meh ah-zoo-DAR ah reh-sohl-VEHR EH-stee
proh-BLEH-mah kohm [proh-DOO-toh/sehr-VEE-soh]?)*

I'm sorry, I didn't catch that. Could you repeat it, please?
Desculpe, eu não entendi. Você poderia repetir, por favor?
*(deh-SKOOL-peh, yoo now ehn-TEHN-dee. voh-SAY poh-deh-REE-ah
peh-peh-TEER, por fah-VOHR?)*

Can you speak more slowly, please?
Você pode falar mais devagar, por favor?
(voh-SAY poh-deh fah-LAR mah-eez deh-vah-GAHR, por fah-VOHR?)

Can you spell that for me, please?
Você pode soletrar isso para mim, por favor?
(voh-SAY poh-deh soh-leh-TRAHR EE-soh pah-rah meh, por fah-VOHR?)

I'll call back later.
Eu vou ligar de volta mais tarde.
(yoo vo LEE-gahr deh VOHL-tah mah-ees TAR-deh)

Thank you for your time.
Obrigado pelo seu tempo.
(oh-bree-GAH-doh peh-loh seh-oo TEHM-poh)

It was nice talking to you.
Foi bom conversar com você.
(foy bohm kohn-ver-SAHR kohm voh-SAY)

Goodbye
Adeus
(ah-DEH-oos)

Have a nice day
Tenha um bom dia
(TEH-nyah oong bohm DEE-ah)

See you soon
Até breve
(ah-teh BREH-veh)

Take care
Cuide-se
(KOO-deh-seh)

Sorry, I dialed the wrong number.
Desculpe, eu discou o número errado.
(deh-SKOOL-peh, yoo dees-KOH-oh oh NOO-meh-roh EH-rah-doh)

Please hold, I'll transfer you to the right department.
Por favor, aguarde, eu vou transferir você para o departamento
correto.
*(por fah-VOHR, ah-goo-AHR-deh, yoo vo trahns-feh-REER voh-SAY
pah-rah oh deh-pahr-tah-MEN-toh koh-REH-toh)*

I'm sorry, the person you are trying to reach is not available.
Desculpe, a pessoa que você está tentando alcançar não está
disponível.
*(deh-SKOOL-peh, ah peh-SOH-ah keh voh-SAY eh-STAH TEHN-tahn-doh
ah-kahn-sahr nown EH-stah dee-SPOH-nee-vehl)*

Can I leave a message?
Posso deixar uma mensagem?
(POH-soh day-SHAHR oong-AH mess-AH-jee?)

I'll have to call you back.

Vou ter que te ligar de volta.

(voh tehr keh teh LEE-gahr deh VOHL-tah)

Thank you for calling.

Obrigado pela ligação.

(oh-bree-GAH-doh peh-lah lee-gah-SOWN)

Can I speak to [name], please?

Posso falar com [nome], por favor?

(POH-soh fah-LAR kohm [NOH-meh], por fah-VOHR?)

Can you give me more information about [topic]?

Você pode me dar mais informações sobre [assunto]?

(voh-SAY poh-deh meh dahr mah-ees een-fohr-mah-SOWNS oh-BREH [ ]?)

DESCRIBING FEELINGS AND EMOTIONS

I feel happy.
Eu me sinto feliz.
(eh-oo may SEEN-too feh-LEESH)

I feel sad.
Eu me sinto triste.
(eh-oo may SEEN-too TREE-steh)

I feel angry.
Eu me sinto irritado.
(eh-oo may SEEN-too ee-ree-TAH-doo)

I feel anxious.
Eu me sinto ansioso.
(eh-oo may SEEN-too ahn-see-OH-soo)

I feel nervous.
Eu estou nervoso.
(eh-oo ehs-TOH ner-VOH-soo)

I feel scared.
Eu estou com medo.
(eh-oo ehs-TOH kohm MEH-doh)

I feel excited.
Eu estou animado.
(eh-oo ehs-TOH ah-nee-MAH-doh)

I feel overwhelmed.
Eu estou sobrecarregado.
(eh-oo ehs-TOH soh-bree-kah-rreh-GAH-doh)

I feel content.
Eu me sinto satisfeito.
(eh-oo may SEEN-too sah-tee-SFEH-toh)

I feel frustrated.
Eu estou frustrado.
(eh-oo ehs-TOH froo-streh-DOO)

I feel disappointed.
Eu estou decepcionado.
(eh-oo ehs-TOH deh-seh-pee-syoh-NAH-doh)

I feel lonely.
Eu me sinto sozinho.
(eh-oo may SEEN-too soh-ZEE-noo)

I feel loved.
Eu me sinto amado.
(eh-oo may SEEN-too ah-MAH-doo)

I feel appreciated.
Eu me sinto apreciado.
(eh-oo may SEEN-too ah-preh-see-AH-doh)

I feel grateful.
Eu me sinto grato.
(eh-oo may SEEN-too GRAH-too)

I feel jealous.
Eu estou com ciúmes.
(eh-oo ehs-TOH kohm see-YOO-mes)

I feel envious.
Eu me sinto invejoso.
(eh-oo may SEEN-too een-veh-JOH-soo)

I feel guilty.
Eu me sinto culpado.
(eh-oo may SEEN-too kool-PAH-doo)

I feel ashamed.
Eu me sinto envergonhado.
(eh-oo may SEEN-too een-veh-roh-NYA-doh)

I feel proud.
Eu me sinto orgulhoso.
(eh-oo may SEEN-too ohr-goo-LHOH-soo)

I feel confident.
Eu me sinto confiante.
(eh-oo may SEEN-too kohn-fee-AHN-teh)

I feel insecure.
Eu me sinto inseguro.
(eh-oo may SEEN-too een-seh-GOO-roo)

I feel inferior.
Eu me sinto inferior.
(eh-oo may SEEN-too een-fee-YOH-roo)

I feel superior.
Eu me sinto superior.
(eh-oo may SEEN-too soo-pee-YOH-roo)

I feel relaxed.
Eu estou relaxado.
(eh-oo ehs-TOH reh-lah-KSAH-doh)

I feel exhausted.
Eu estou exausto.
(eh-oo ehs-TOH eh-SOWS-toh)

I feel energized.
Eu me sinto energizado.
(eh-oo may SEEN-too en-ehr-jee-ZAH-doh)

I feel motivated.
Eu estou motivado.
(eh-oo ehs-TOH moh-tee-VAH-doh)

I feel inspired.
Eu me sinto inspirado.
(eh-oo may SEEN-too een-spee-RAH-doh)

I feel bored.
Eu estou entediado.
(eh-oo ehs-TOH ehn-teh-jee-AH-doh)

DISCUSSING HEALTH AND WELL-BEING

I try to eat a balanced diet to maintain my health.
Eu tento comer uma dieta equilibrada para manter minha saúde.
(ehu ten-too ko-MER oon-a dee-ET-a eh-kee-lee-BRA-da pa-ra man-TEER MEE-nha sa-OO-de)

I go for a run every morning to keep fit.
Eu corro todas as manhãs para me manter em forma.
(ehu KO-ro to-das as ma-NHAS pa-ra me man-TER em FOR-ma)

I try to get at least 8 hours of sleep every night.
Eu tento dormir pelo menos 8 horas todas as noites.
(ehu ten-too dor-MEER PE-lo me-nos OI-to ho-ras to-das as NOI-tes)

I've been feeling a bit under the weather lately.
Eu tenho me sentido um pouco indisposto(a) ultimamente.
(ehu TE-nho me sen-TI-do oom PO-co in-dis-POS-to(o) UL-ti-ma-MEN-te)

I've been experiencing some back pain recently.
Eu tenho sentido dor nas costas ultimamente.
(ehu TE-nho sen-TI-do dor nas KOSS-tas UL-ti-ma-MEN-te)

I've been feeling a bit stressed lately.
Eu tenho me sentido um pouco estressado(a) ultimamente.
(ehu TE-nho me sen-TI-do oom PO-co es-TRESS-a-do(o) UL-ti-ma-MEN-te)

I try to practice mindfulness to reduce stress.
Eu tento praticar mindfulness para reduzir o estresse.
(ehu ten-too pra-TEE-car MIND-ful-ness pa-ra re-du-ZEER o es-TRESS-e)

I make sure to take breaks throughout the day to stretch and move my body.
Eu me certifico de fazer pausas ao longo do dia para esticar e mover o meu corpo.
(ehu me cer-tee-fee-koo de fa-ZER PAU-sas a-o LON-go do DIA pa-ra es-tee-CAR e mo-VER o meu COR-po)

I take vitamins and supplements to support my immune system.
Eu tomo vitaminas e suplementos para apoiar meu sistema imunológico.
(ehu TO-mo vee-ta-MEE-nas e su-ple-MEN-tos pa-ra a-POI-ar MEU sis-TE-ma i-mu-no-LÓ-gi-co)

I've been trying to cut down on my sugar intake.
Eu tenho tentado reduzir a minha ingestão de açúcar.
(ehu TE-nho ten-TA-do re-du-ZEER a MI-nha in-GES-tão de a-SSOO-kar)

I've been experiencing some digestive issues lately.
Eu tenho tido alguns problemas digestivos ultimamente.
(ehu TE-nho TI-do al-GUNS pro-BLE-mas di-ges-TEE-vos UL-ti-ma-MEN-te)

I go to the gym regularly to stay in shape.
Eu vou à academia regularmente para me manter em forma.
(ehu VO-oo a a-CA-de-mi-a re-gu-lar-MEN-te pa-ra me man-TER em FOR-ma)

I like to practice yoga to improve my flexibility and reduce stress.
Eu gosto de praticar yoga para melhorar minha flexibilidade e reduzir o estresse.
(ehu GOS-to de pra-TEE-car YO-ga pa-ra me-LHO-rar MEE-nha fle-ksi-bi-li-DA-de e re-du-ZEER o es-TRESS-e)

I try to limit my alcohol consumption to avoid health problems.
Eu tento limitar meu consumo de álcool para evitar problemas de saúde.
(ehu ten-too li-MI-tar MEU con-su-MO de ÁL-co-ol pa-ra e-vi-TAR pro-BLE-mas de sa-OO-de)

I've been experiencing some joint pain lately.
Eu tenho sentido dor nas articulações ultimamente.
(ehu TE-nho sen-TI-do dor nas ar-ti-cu-la-ÇÕES UL-ti-ma-MEN-te)

I go for a walk every evening to relax and clear my mind.
Eu vou dar uma caminhada todas as noites para relaxar e limpar minha mente.
(ehu VO-oo dar OO-ma ka-mi-NA-da to-das as NOI-tes pa-ra re-la-xar e LIM-par MEE-nha MEN-te)

I try to incorporate more fruits and vegetables into my diet for better nutrition.
Eu tento incorporar mais frutas e legumes em minha dieta para uma melhor nutrição.
(ehu ten-too in-cor-por-CAR mais FROO-tas e le-GU-mes em MEE-nha dee-ET-a pa-ra oo-ma me-LHOR nu-tri-ÇÃO)

I've been trying to quit smoking for a while now.
Eu tenho tentado parar de fumar há um tempo.
(ehu TE-nho ten-TA-do pa-RAR de foo-MAR a-oom tem-po)

I make sure to wear sunscreen when I go outside to protect my skin.
Eu me certifico de usar protetor solar quando saio para proteger minha pele.
(ehu me cer-tee-fee-koo de oo-SAR pro-te-TOR so-LAR QUAN-do SA-io pa-ra pro-te-JER MEE-nha PE-le)

I like to meditate in the morning to start my day off on the right foot.
Eu gosto de meditar de manhã para começar o dia com o pé direito.
(ehu GOS-to de me-di-TAR de ma-NHÃ pa-ra co-ME-çar o DIA com o PE di-REI-to)

I've been feeling a bit anxious lately and it's affecting my sleep.
Eu tenho me sentido um pouco ansioso*(a)* ultimamente e isso está afetando meu sono.
(ehu TE-nho me sen-TI-do oom PO-co an-see-O-so(o) UL-ti-ma-MEN-te e ISSO es-TÁ a-fe-TAN-do MEU SO-no)

I make sure to get regular check-ups with my doctor to monitor my health.

Eu me certifico de fazer check-ups regulares com meu médicopara monitorar minha saúde.

(ehu me cer-tee-fee-koo de FA-zer chek-UPS re-gu-LA-res com MEU MÉ-di-co pa-ra mo-ni-to-RAR MEE-nha sa-OO-de)

I try to get at least 7 hours of sleep every night to feel well-rested.

Eu tento dormir pelo menos 7 horas todas as noites para me sentir descansado(a).

(ehu ten-to dor-MEER PE-lo me-NOS SE-te HOR-as to-das as NOI-tes pa-ra me sen-TIR des-can-sa-do(a))

I've been feeling a bit under the weather lately, I might be getting a cold.

Eu tenho me sentido um pouco mal ultimamente, talvez eu esteja pegando um resfriado.

(ehu TE-nho me sen-TI-do oom PO-co mal UL-ti-ma-MEN-te, tal-VEZ eus-TA-ja pe-GAN-do oom res-fri-A-do)

I like to take breaks throughout the day to stretch and move my body.

Eu gosto de fazer pausas durante o dia para esticar e movimentar meu corpo.

(ehu GOS-to de fa-ZER PAU-sas du-ran-TE o DIA pa-ra es-ti-CAR e mo-vi-men-TAR MEE-nho COR-po)

I make sure to stay hydrated by drinking plenty of water throughout the day.

Eu me certifico de me manter hidratado*(a)* bebendo bastante água durante o dia.

(ehu me cer-tee-fee-koo de me man-TER i-dra-ta-DO(a) be-BEN-do bas-TAN-te ÁGUA du-ran-te o DIA)

I like to set fitness goals for myself to stay motivated and track my progress.

Eu gosto de definir metas de fitness para mim mesmo*(a)* para me manter motivado*(a)* e acompanhar meu progresso.

(ehu GOS-to de de-fi-NIR ME-tas de FIT-ness pa-ra MIM meS-mo(a) pa-ra me man-TER mo-ti-VA-do(a) e a-com-PAN-har MEE-u pro-GRES-so)

I try to practice good hygiene habits to prevent the spread of germs and illness.

Eu tento praticar bons hábitos de higiene para prevenir a propagação de germes e doenças.

(ehu ten-to pra-TEE-car bons Á-bi-tos de hi-GI-e-ne pa-ra pre-ve-NIR a pro-pa-ga-ÇÃO de JER-mes e DO-en-ças)

I always make sure to warm up before exercising to prevent injury.

Eu sempre me certifico de aquecer antes de fazer exercícios para prevenir lesões.

(ehu SEM-pre me cer-tee-fee-koo de a-que-CER an-TES de fa-ZER exer-CÍ-cios pa-ra pre-ve-NIR le-SÕES)

DESCRIBING JOBS AND PROFESSIONS

I work in the tech industry.
Eu trabalho na indústria de tecnologia.
(ayoo trah-bah-lyoh nah een-doo-stree-ya jee teh-noh-loh-ZHEE-ah)

I'm a lawyer.
Eu sou advogado.
(ayoo soh ah-dvo-GAH-doo)

I'm a doctor.
Eu sou médico.
(ayoo soh MAY-dee-koo)

I'm a teacher.
Eu sou professor.
(ayoo soh proh-fes-SOR)

I'm an accountant.
Eu sou contador.
(ayoo soh kohn-TAH-dohr)

I'm an engineer.
Eu sou engenheiro.
(ayoo soh en-jeh-NHEY-roh)

I work in finance.
Eu trabalho em finanças.
(ayoo trah-bah-lyoh ehn fee-nahn-SAHSH)

I'm a journalist.
Eu sou jornalista.
(ayoo soh zhor-nah-LEES-tah)

I'm a musician.
Eu sou músico.
(ayoo soh MOO-see-koo)

I'm an artist.
Eu sou artista.
(ayoo soh ahr-TEES-tah)

I'm a chef.
Eu sou chef de cozinha.
(ayoo soh shehf deh koh-ZEE-nyah)

I work in marketing.
Eu trabalho em marketing.
(ayoo trah-bah-lyoh ehn mahr-keht-eeng)

I'm a salesperson.
Eu sou vendedor.
(ayoo soh vehn-deh-DOR)

I'm a software developer.
Eu sou desenvolvedor de software.
(ayoo soh den-vohl-vey-DOHR deh sohf-TWAH-reh)

I work in customer service.
Eu trabalho no atendimento ao cliente.
(ayoo trah-bah-lyoh noh ah-ten-DEE-men-toh ow klee-EHN-teh)

I'm a graphic designer.
Eu sou designer gráfico.
(ayoo soh dez-ee-NYEH-r grah-fee-koo)

I'm a writer.
Eu sou escritor.
(ayoo soh ess-kree-TOR)

I'm a consultant.
Eu sou consultor.
(ayoo soh kon-sool-TOR)

I work in human resources.
Eu trabalho em recursos humanos.
(ayoo trah-bah-lyoh ehn reh-soo-SOH-eez oo-MAH-noos)

I'm a project manager.
Eu sou gerente de projetos.
(ayoo soh zheh-REHN-teh deh proh-JEH-tohs)

I'm a social worker.
Eu sou assistente social.
(ayoo soh ah-see-STEN-teh soh-SHYAL)

I work in public relations.
Eu trabalho em relações públicas.
(ayoo trah-bah-lyoh ehn reh-lah-SEE-ownsh POO-blee-cas)

I'm a nurse.
Eu sou enfermeiro.
(ayoo soh en-fehr-MEY-roh)

I'm a scientist.
Eu sou cientista.
(ayoo soh see-EN-teesh-tah)

I'm a researcher.
Eu sou pesquisador.
(ayoo soh peh-skee-zah-DOHR)

I'm a therapist.
Eu sou terapeuta.
(ayoo soh teh-rah-PEH-tah)

I work in hospitality.
Eu trabalho na área de hospitalidade.
(ayoo trah-bah-lyoh nah ah-REE-ah deh oh-spee-tah-lee-DAH-deh)

I'm a real estate agent.
Eu sou corretor de imóveis.
(ayoo soh kor-reh-TOHR deh ee-MOH-veysh)

I'm a financial advisor.
Eu sou consultor financeiro.
(ayoo soh kon-sool-TOR fee-nahn-SEE-roh)

I'm a pharmacist.
Eu sou farmacêutico.
(ayoo soh fahr-mah-SEW-tee-koh)

GIVING AND RECEIVING INSTRUCTIONS

Please do this.
Por favor, faça isso.
(pohr fah-VOHR, FAH-sah EE-soh)

Could you please do this?
Você poderia fazer isso, por favor?
(voh-SEH poh-deh-REE-ah fah-ZEHR EE-soh, pohr fah-VOHR)

Would you mind doing this?
Você se importaria em fazer isso?
(voh-SEH see eem-pohr-TEE-AH ehm fah-ZEHR EE-soh?)

I'd like you to do this.
Eu gostaria que você fizesse isso.
(EH-oo gohs-TAH-ree-ah keh voh-SEH fee-ZEHS-see EE-soh.)

Can you do this for me?
Você pode fazer isso para mim?
(voh-SEH POH-deh fah-ZEHR EE-soh PAH-rah meem?)

It's important that you do this.
É importante que você faça isso.
(EH eem-pohr-TAHN-teh keh voh-SEH FAH-sah EE-soh.)

Don't forget to do this.
Não se esqueça de fazer isso.
(NA-o sey es-KEH-sah deh fah-ZEHR EE-soh.)

Make sure you do this.
Certifique-se de fazer isso.
(sehr-tee-EE-keh-seh deh fah-ZEHR EE-soh.)

You need to do this.
Você precisa fazer isso.
(voh-SEH preh-SEE-sah fah-ZEHR EE-soh.)

This is what you should do.
Isso é o que você deve fazer.
(EE-soh eh oh keh voh-SEH DEH-veh fah-ZEHR.)

Sure, I can do that.
Claro, eu posso fazer isso.
(KLAH-roh, EH-oo POHS-soh fah-ZEHR EE-soh.)

Of course, I'll do it right away.
É claro, eu farei isso imediatamente.
*(EH KLAH-roh, EH-oo fah-REH-ee EE-soh
ee-meh-dee-ah-tah-MEHN-tee.)*

Absolutely, I'll get right on it.
Com certeza, eu vou fazer isso agora.
(kohm sehr-TEE-zah, EH-oo VOH fah-ZEHR EE-soh NA-oh-rah.)

No problem, I can do that.
Nenhum problema, eu posso fazer isso.
(NEHN-yoom proh-BLEH-mah, EH-oo POHS-soh fah-ZEHR EE-soh.)

I understand, I'll do it.
Eu entendo, eu farei isso.
(EH-oo ehn-TEN-doh, EH-oo fah-REH-ee EE-soh.)

Okay, I'll make sure to do that.
Ok, eu vou ter certeza de fazer isso.
(OH-keh, EH-oo VOH tehr sehr-TEE-zah deh fah-ZEHR EE-soh.)

Consider it done.
Considere feito.
(kohn-SEE-deh-reh FEH-to)

I'll take care of it.
Eu vou cuidar disso.
(EH-oo VOH koo-ee-DAHR DEE-soh.)

Right away, I'll do it.
Imediatamente, eu farei isso.
(ee-meh-dee-ah-TAH-mehn-tee, EH-oo fah-REH-ee EE-soh.)

Yes, I can do that for you.
Sim, eu posso fazer isso por você.
(seem, EH-oo POHS-soh fah-ZEHR EE-soh pohr voh-SEH.)

Can you explain that again?
Você pode explicar isso de novo?
(voh-SEH POH-deh eks-plee-KAHR EE-soh deh NO-voh?)

Could you give me more detail on that?
Você poderia me dar mais detalhes sobre isso?
(voh-SEH poh-DEH-ree-ah meh DAHR mohs deh-TAH-lyehs soo-BRE EE-soh?)

Just to clarify, you want me to do this?
Só para esclarecer, você quer que eu faça isso?
(soh PAH-rah ehsklah-REH-sehr, voh-SEH kehr keh EH-oo FAH-sah EE-soh?)

Do you mean that I should do this first?
Você quer dizer que eu devo fazer isso primeiro?
(voh-SEH kehr deh-ZEHR keh EH-oo DEH-voh fah-ZEHR EE-soh prhee-MEH-roh?)

Sorry, I missed that part, can you repeat it?
Desculpe, eu perdi essa parte, você pode repetir?
(deh-skool-peh, EH-oo PEHR-dee EHS-sah PAHR-teh, voh-SEH POH-deh reh-peh-TEER?)

Can you give me an example of what you mean?
Você pode me dar um exemplo do que quer dizer?
(voh-SEH POH-deh meh DAHR oom ehks-EHM-ploh doh keh KEHR DEE-zer?)

Can you explain the reasoning behind that?
Você pode explicar a razão por trás disso?
(voh-SEH POH-deh eks-plee-KAHR ah rah-ZAHW pohr trahz DEE-soh?)

Can you show me how to do this?
Você pode me mostrar como fazer isso?
(voh-SEH POH-deh meh shoh-WAH koh-moh fah-ZEHR EE-soh?)

EXPRESSING UNCERTAINTY OR PROBABILITY

It's hard to say.
É difícil dizer.
(eh dee-fee-SEEL dee-ZEHR.)

I'm not sure.
Não tenho certeza.
(now TEHN-yoo sehr-TEH-zah.)

I don't know for certain.
Não sei com certeza.
(now say kohm sehr-TEH-zah.)

It could go either way.
Pode ir de qualquer maneira.
(POH-dee eer deh KEH-yoo-ehr mah-NAY-rah.)

It's anyone's guess.
É um palpite de qualquer um.
(eh oong pahl-PEE-teh deh KEH-yoo-ahl KWAHL-kair oong.)

It's a toss-up.
É uma questão de sorte.
(eh oong-ah keh-STOW(n) deh SOHR-chee.)

There's a chance that...
Existe uma chance de que...
(eh-SHEES-teh OO-mah SHAWN-see deh keh...)

There's a possibility that...
Existe uma possibilidade de que...
(eh-SHEES-teh OO-mah poh-see-bee-lee-DAH-deh deh keh...)

It's not out of the question.
Não está fora de cogitação.
(now eh-STAH foh-rah deh koh-jee-tah-SOW.)

It's a long shot.
É difícil de acontecer.
(eh dee-fee-SEEL dee ah-kawn-TEH-sehr.)

I'm not convinced.
Não estou convencido.
(now eh-STOW kohn-veh(n)-SEE-doo.)

It's too soon to tell.
É cedo demais para dizer.
(eh SEH-doo deh-MAH-eez pah-rah dee-ZEHR.)

It's up in the air.
Está no ar.
(eh-STAH noo ahr.)

It's uncertain.
É incerto.
(eh een-SER-too.)

I have my doubts.
Eu tenho minhas dúvidas.
(eh-oo TEH-nyoo MEE-nhahs DOO-vee-dahs.)

It's questionable.
É questionável.
(eh keh-stee-oh-NAH-vehl.)

It's debatable.
É discutível.
(eh dees-koo-TEE-vehl.)

I'm on the fence about it.
Estou em cima do muro em relação a isso.
(eh-STOH ehn SEE-pah doh MOO-roo ehn reh-lah-SOW ah EE-soo.)

It's a gamble.
É um jogo de azar.
(eh oong ZHO-go deh ah-ZAHR.)

It's not a sure thing.
Não é algo certo.
(now eh AHL-goo SEHR-too.)

It's not guaranteed.
Não é garantido.
(now eh gah-rahn-TEE-doo.)

It's possible, but unlikely.
É possível, mas improvável.
(eh POH-see-vehl, mahs een-proh-VAH-vehl.)

It's a remote possibility.
É uma possibilidade remota.
(eh oong-ah poh-see-bee-lee-DAH-deh reh-MOH-tah.)

It's more likely than not.
É mais provável do que não.
(eh mah-eez proh-VAH-vehl doh keh now.)

It's probable.
É provável.
(eh proh-VAH-vehl.)

There's a good chance that...
Há uma boa chance de que...
(ah OO-mah BOH-ah SHAWN-see deh keh...)

It's highly likely.
É altamente provável.
(eh ahl-TAH-men-teh proh-VAH-vehl.)

It's almost certain.
É quase certo.
(eh KWAA-zee SEHR-too.)

I'm fairly confident.
Estou bastante confiante.
(eh-STOH BAH-stah(n)-teh kohn-fee-YAHN-teh.)

SKILLS

I am experienced in...
Eu tenho experiência em...
(eh-oo TEH-nyoo eks-peh-ree-EN-see-ah ehm...)

I am qualified and capable of...
Eu sou qualificado e capaz de...
(eh-oo sow kwah-lee-fee-KAH-doh ee kah-PAHJ dee...)

I am highly proficient in...
Eu sou altamente proficiente em...
(eu sow awl-tuh-MEN-tee proh-fee-SEN-tee emm...)

I possess exceptional expertise in...
Eu possuo uma expertise excepcional em...
(eu poh-SOO-oh oon-ah ex-pehr-TEE-zhee ee-shay-see-o-NAWL emm)

Communication skills
Habilidade de comunicação
(ha-bi-li-DA-de de ko-mu-ni-ka-sa-o)

Problem-solving skills
Habilidade de resolução de problemas
(ha-bi-li-DA-de de re-so-lu-sa-o de pro-ble-mas)

Teamwork
Trabalho em equipe
(tra-ba-lyo em e-ki-pe)

Time management
Gerenciamento de tempo
(ge-ren-ci-a-men-to de tem-po)

Leadership
Liderança
(li-de-ran-sa)

Customer service
Atendimento ao cliente
(a-ten-di-men-to a-o kli-en-te)

Creativity
Criatividade
(kri-a-ti-vi-da-de)

Attention to detail
Atenção aos detalhes
(a-ten-sa-o a-os de-ta-lhes)

Sales skills
Habilidade de vendas
(ha-bi-li-DA-de de ven-das)

Marketing skills
Habilidade de marketing
(ha-bi-li-DA-de de mar-ke-ting)

Financial management
Gestão financeira
(ges-ta-o fi-nan-cei-ra)

Project management
Gerenciamento de projetos
(ge-ren-ci-a-men-to de pro-je-tos)

Public speaking
Falar em público
(fa-lar em pu-bli-co)

Analytical skills
Habilidade analítica
(ha-bi-li-DA-de a-na-li-ti-ca)

Negotiation skills
Habilidade de negociação
(ha-bi-li-DA-de de ne-go-ci-a-sa-o)

Critical thinking
Pensamento crítico
(pen-sa-men-to kri-ti-co)

Technical skills
Habilidade técnica
(ha-bi-li-DA-de te-ki-ni-ka)

Interpersonal skills
Habilidade interpessoal
(ha-bi-li-DA-de in-ter-pe-so-al)

Digital literacy
Alfabetização digital
(al-fa-be-ti-za-sa-o di-gi-tal)

Strategic thinking
Pensamento estratégico
(pen-sa-men-to es-tra-te-gi-co)

Decision-making
Tomada de decisão
(to-ma-da de de-ci-sa-o)

Coaching
Coaching
(ko-ching)

Conflict resolution
Resolução de conflitos
(re-so-lu-sa-o de kon-fli-tos)

Multitasking
Multitarefa
(mul-ti-ta-re-fa)

Problem analysis
Análise de problemas
(a-na-li-ze de pro-ble-mas)

FAMILY

How many siblings do you have?
Quantos irmãos você tem?
(KWAN-tohs eer-MAN-yos VOH-seh tehn)

Are you the oldest, middle, or youngest child?
Você é o filho mais velho, do meio ou o mais novo?
(VOH-seh eh oh FEE-yoh mahys VEL-yoh, doh MAY-oh oo oh mahys NOH-voh)

What are your parents' occupations?
Qual é a profissão dos seus pais?
(KAHL eh ah proh-fiss-YOWN dohs seh-oos pie-ees)

Do you have any step-siblings or half-siblings?
Você tem irmãos de meio ou de outra união?
(VOH-seh teh eer-MAN-yos dee MAY-oh oo dee OH-trah oo-NYOWN)

What is your family's cultural background?
Qual é a origem cultural da sua família?
(KAHL eh ah oh-REE-zhehng kool-tchoo-AHL dah SOO-ah fah-MEE-lyah)

Do you have any family traditions?
Você tem alguma tradição familiar?
(VOH-seh teh-M alg-OOM-ah trah-dee-SOWN fah-mee-LYAH)

What is your relationship like with your parents?
(Como é a sua relação com seus pais?
(KOH-moh eh ah SOO-ah reh-lah-see-OWN kohm seh-oos pie-ees)

Do you have any nieces or nephews?
Você tem sobrinhos?
(VOH-seh teh SOH-bree-nyoos)

Are your grandparents still alive?
(Seus avós ainda estão vivos?
(seh-oos ah-VOHS EEN-dah ehs-TAH-oh VEE-vohs)

Where do your parents or grandparents come from?
De onde são seus pais ou avós?
(dee OHN-deh sah-o seh-oos pie-ees oo ah-VOHS)

Do you have any family members who live abroad?
Você tem algum parente que mora fora do país?
(VOH-seh teh ah-GOOM pah-REN-chee keh MOH-rah FOH-rah doh pah-EESS)

What is your family's religion or spiritual beliefs?
Qual é a religião ou crença espiritual da sua família?
(KAHL eh ah ree-lee-ZHOW oh krehn-sah ess-pee-ree-TWAHL dah SOO-ah fah-MEE-lyah)

How often do you see your extended family members?
Com que frequência você vê seus parentes distantes?
(kohm keh free-KWEN-see-ah VOH-seh veh seh-oos pah-REN-tehs dee-STAHN-tees)

Do you have any family pets?
Você tem animais de estimação?
(VOH-seh teh ah-NEE-mahys dee ehs-tee-mah-SOWN)

Who is the family member you are closest to?
Qual é o membro da família com quem você tem mais proximidade?
(KAL eh ooh MEM-broh dah fah-MEE-lyah kohm kehm VOH-seh teh mahys proh-kshee-MEE-dah-gee)

Do you have a family crest or coat of arms?
Você tem um brasão de família?
(VOH-seh teh oong brah-SOWN dee fah-MEE-lyah)

What is your family's favorite cuisine or dish?
Qual é a culinária ou prato favorito da sua família?
(KAHL eh ah koo-lee-NAH-ree-ah oo PRAH-toh fah-voh-REE-toh dah SOO-ah fah-MEE-lyah)

Are there any family members who are artists or musicians?

Há algum membro da família que seja artista ou músico?

(AH ahl-goom MEM-broh dah fah-MEE-lyah keh SEH-jah ahch-TEES-tah oo MOO-zee-koh)

Do you have any family heirlooms or sentimental objects?

Você tem algum objeto de família passado de geração em geração ou algo que tenha valor sentimental?

(VOH-seh teh ah-GOOM oh-beh-toh dee fah-MEE-lyah pah-SAH-doh deh jeh-rah-SOWN ehm jeh-rah-SOWN oo AHL-goh keh TEHN-yah VAH-lor sen-tee-men-TAHL)

What is the most important lesson you have learned from your family?

Qual é a lição mais importante que você aprendeu com sua família?

(KAHL eh ah lee-SOWN mahys eem-pohr-TAHN-teh keh VOH-seh ah-prehn-DEH-oo kohm SOO-ah fah-MEE-lyah)

Do you have any family members who have served in the military?

Você tem algum parente que tenha servido nas forças armadas?

(VOH-seh teh ah-GOOM pah-REN-chee keh TEHN-yah sehr-VEE-doh nahs FOHR-sess ar-MAH-dahs)

What is the biggest challenge your family has faced?

Qual foi o maior desafio que a sua família enfrentou?

(KAHL foh-ee oh mah-YOR deh-sah-FEE-oh keh ah SOO-ah fah-MEE-lyah en-frehn-TOH)

Are there any family members who are entrepreneurs or business owners?

Há membros da família que são empreendedores ou donos de empresas?

(AH MEM-brohs dah fah-MEE-lyah keh soh ehm-pree-en-deh-DOR-esh oo DOH-noos deh em-preh-ZAHs)

What is your family's stance on important social issues?

Qual é a posição da sua família sobre questões sociais importantes?

(KAHL eh ah po-see-SOWN dah SOO-ah fah-MEE-lyah soh-breh kehs-tee-OHNS soh-see-AHYS eem-pohr-TAHN-tehs)

Do you have any family members who are educators or involved in academia?

Você tem membros da família que são educadores ou envolvidos com a academia?

(VOH-seh teh MEHM-brohss dah fah-MEE-lyah keh soh eh-doo-kah-DOR-ess oo ehn-vohl-VEE-dohs kohm ah kah-DEH-mee-ah)

What is your family's religious or spiritual background?

Qual é a formação religiosa ou espiritual da sua família?

(KAHL eh ah for-mah-SOWN reh-lee-GEE-yo-sah oo eh-spee-ree-TOO-ahl dah SOO-ah fah-MEE-lyah)

Are there any family members who are involved in charitable or volunteer work?

Há membros da família envolvidos em trabalho voluntário ou de caridade?

(AH MEM-brohs dah fah-MEE-lyah ehn-vohl-VEE-dohs ehm trah-bah-LYOH vol-un-TAH-ree-oh oo deh kah-ree-DAH-jee)

What is the most memorable family vacation or trip you have taken together?

Qual foi a viagem ou férias em família mais memorável que vocês fizeram juntos?

(KAHL foh-ee ah vee-AH-jehm oo FEH-ree-ahs ehm fah-MEE-lyah mahys mehm-oh-RAH-vehl keh VOH-sehss fee-ZEH-rahm JOON-tohs)

Do you have any family members who have achieved something noteworthy or remarkable?

Você tem algum membro da família que realizou algo notável ou digno de nota?

(VOH-seh teh ah-GOOM MEM-broh dah fah-MEE-lyah keh heh-ah-LEE-zoh AL-goh noh-TAH-vehl oo DEE-nyoh deh NOH-tah)

What is your family's opinion on marriage and relationships?

Qual é a opinião da sua família sobre casamento e relacionamentos?

(KAHL eh ah oh-pee-NYOHN dah SOO-ah fah-MEE-lyah soo-breh kah-sah-MEN-toh ee reh-lah-see-oh-na-MEN-toos)

Do you have any family traditions or customs that are unique to your family?
Vocês têm alguma tradição ou costume familiar que seja único?
(VOH-sehss teh-ehm ah-GOO-mah trah-dee-SOWN oo kohs-TOO-mee fah-mee-LYAHRR keh SEH-jah oo-NEE-koo)

Who in your family is the best storyteller?
Quem na sua família é o melhor contador de histórias?
(KEHM nah SOO-ah fah-MEE-lyah eh oh meh-LYOHR kohn-TAH-dohr deh HISS-toh-ree-ahs)

Do you have any family members who are skilled in a particular craft or hobby?
Você tem membros da família que são habilidosos em alguma arte ou hobby?
(VOH-seh teh MEHM-brohss dah fah-MEE-lyah keh soh ah-bee-lee-DOH-sooss ehm ah-GOO-mah AR-tee oo HO-bee)

What is the most interesting fact about your family history?
Qual é o fato mais interessante sobre a história da sua família?
(KAHL eh oh FAH-toh mahys een-teh-ress-AHN-tee soo-BREH ah his-TOH-ree-ah dah SOO-ah fah-MEE-lyah)

Are there any family recipes or dishes that have been passed down through generations?
Existem receitas ou pratos na sua família que foram passados de geração em geração?
(ehks-ee-STEHM reh-SEH-ee-tahs oo PRAH-toos nah SOO-ah fah-MEE-lyah keh foh-RAHM pah-SAH-dohss deh jeh-rah-SOWN ehm jeh-rah-SOWN)

What is your family's stance on education and lifelong learning?
Qual é a opinião da sua família sobre educação e aprendizado ao longo da vida?
(KAHL eh ah oh-pee-NYOHN dah SOO-ah fah-MEE-lyah soo-breh eh-doo-kah-SOWN ee ah-prehn-JEE-zah-doo ah LOHN-goh dah VEE-dah)

Do you have any family members who have served in the military or law enforcement?
Você tem membros da família que já serviram nas forças armadas ou na polícia?
(VOH-seh teh MEHM-brohss dah fah-MEE-lyah keh jah sehr-VEE-rahm nahss FOHRS-ess ahr-MAH-dahss oo nah poh-LEE-see-ah)

What is the most challenging experience your family has faced together?
Qual foi a experiência mais desafiadora que a sua família já enfrentou junta?
(KAHL foh-ee ah eks-peh-ree-NSEE-ah mahys deh-sah-fee-AH-doh-rah keh ah SOO-ah fah-MEE-lyah jah ehn-frehn-TOH jOON-tah)

Do you have any family members who have migrated or moved to a different country?
Você tem membros da família que migraram ou se mudaram para outro país?
(VOH-seh teh MEHM-brohss dah fah-MEE-lyah keh mee-grah-rahm oo seh moo-DAH-rahm pah-rah OOH-troh pah-EESS)

What is your family's opinion on politics and government?
Qual é a opinião da sua família sobre política e governo?
(KAHL eh ah oh-pee-NYOHN dah SOO-ah fah-MEE-lyah soo-breh poh-LEE-tee-kah ee go-VEHR-noo)

Do you have any family traditions or customs that are unique to your family?
Você tem alguma tradição ou costume de família que seja única?
(VOH-seh teh-ehm ahl-GOO-mah trah-dee-SOWN oo koh-STOO-mee deh fah-MEE-lyah keh SEH-jah oo-NEE-kah)

Has your family ever experienced a natural disaster or emergency situation?
Sua família já passou por alguma situação de desastre natural ou emergência?
(SOO-ah fah-MEE-lyah jah pah-SOW pohr ahl-GOO-mah see-too-ah-SOWN deh deh-SAHS-treh nah-TOO-ral oo eh-mehr-ZHEHN-see-ah)

What is your family's opinion on religion and spirituality?
Qual é a opinião da sua família sobre religião e espiritualidade?
(KAHL eh ah oh-pee-NYOHN dah SOO-ah fah-MEE-lyah soo-breh reh-lee-JEE-own ee eh-spee-ree-too-ah-lee-DAH-jee)

Are there any family members who have achieved notable accomplishments or made significant contributions to society?
Existem membros da família que alcançaram realizações notáveis ou fizeram contribuições significativas para a sociedade?
(ehks-ee-STEHM MEHM-brohss dah fah-MEE-lyah keh ahl-kahn-SAH-rahm reh-lee-zah-SOWNSS noh-TAH-vee-ays oo fee-ZEH-rahm kon-tree-boo-ee-SOWNSS ee-see-nee-fee-KAH-tivahs pah-rah ah soh-see-eh-DAHD-jee)

What is your family's favorite way to spend time together?
Qual é a maneira favorita da sua família de passar o tempo juntos?
(KAHL eh ah mah-NEH-rah fah-voh-REE-tah dah SOO-ah fah-MEE-lyah jee pah-SAH oh TEHM-poo JOON-toos)

Do you have any family members who have overcome significant obstacles or challenges in their lives?
Você tem membros da família que superaram obstáculos ou desafios significativos em suas vidas?
(VOH-seh teh MEHM-brohss dah fah-MEE-lyah keh soo-peh-rah-rahm ohb-stah-KOO-loos oo deh-sah-fee-OHS see-nee-fee-KAH-teevohs ehm SOO-ahs VEE-dahs)

What is the most important lesson or value that your family has taught you?
Qual é a lição ou valor mais importante que a sua família te ensinou?
(KAHL eh ah lee-SON oh VAH-lohr mahys eem-pohr-TAHN-tcheh keh ah SOO-ah fah-MEE-lyah cheh ehn-see-NOH-oh)

BUSINESS NEGOTIATION

Let's start with the initial proposal.
Vamos começar com a proposta inicial.
(VAH-moosh koh-MEH-sahr kohm ah proh-POS-tah een-ee-SEE-ahl)

We need to identify our common interests.
Precisamos identificar nossos interesses comuns.
(pre-see-MOHSH ee-den-tee-fee-KAHR NOH-soos een-ter-ESS-es KOH-moosh)

Can we find a middle ground that works for both parties?
Podemos encontrar um meio-termo que funcione para ambas as partes?
(poh-DEH-moosh een-kohn-TRAHR ooh MEH-yoh TEHR-moh kee foon-see-OH-nee PAH-rah AM-bahs ahs PAHR-tes)

Let's discuss the timeline for implementation.
Vamos discutir o cronograma para implementação.
(VAH-moosh dees-KOO-teer oh kroh-noh-GRAH-mah PAH-rah een-pleh-men-tah-SAHW)

We need to consider the budget constraints.
Precisamos considerar as restrições orçamentárias.
(pre-see-MOHSH kohn-see-deh-RAHR ahs rehs-tree-SEE-ohsh ohr-sah-men-TAH-ree-ahsh)

Can we negotiate on the payment terms?
Podemos negociar os termos de pagamento?
(poh-DEH-moosh ne-go-see-AHR ohs TEHR-mohs deh pah-gah-MEN-too)

Let's discuss the scope of the project.
Vamos discutir o escopo do projeto.
(VAH-moosh dees-KOO-teer oh EH-skoh-poh doh proh-JEH-to)

We need to clarify the roles and responsibilities of each party.
Precisamos esclarecer os papéis e responsabilidades de cada parte.
*(pre-see-MOHSH es-kla-REH-ser ohs pah-PEYS ee
rehs-pohn-see-bi-lee-DAH-deh KA-da PAR-teh)*

Can we discuss the potential risks and challenges?
Podemos discutir os riscos e desafios potenciais?
*(poh-DEH-moosh dees-KOO-teer ohs RIS-kohs ee deh-sah-FEE-ohs
poh-ten-see-AH-ees)*

Let's explore options for mutual benefit.
Vamos explorar opções para benefício mútuo.
*(VAH-moosh eks-ploh-RAR oh-PSOHNS PAH-rah beh-ne-FEE-see-oh
MOO-too)*

We need to review and finalize the contract.
Precisamos rever e finalizar o contrato.
(pre-see-MOHSH REH-vehr ee fee-nah-lee-ZAHR oh kon-TRAH-to)

Can we agree on the terms and conditions?
Podemos concordar com os termos e condições?
*(poh-DEH-moosh kohn-kor-DAHR kohm ohs TEHR-mohs ee
kohn-dee-SEE-ohsh)*

We need to negotiate a win-win situation.
Precisamos negociar uma situação em que ambas as partes saiam
ganhando.
*(pre-see-MOHSH ne-go-see-AHR OO-mah see-too-ah-SEE-ow eh kee
AM-bahs ahs PAHR-tes SAH-yahm GA-nyahn-doo)*

Can we discuss the deliverables and deadlines?
Podemos discutir as entregas e prazos?
(poh-DEH-moosh dees-KOO-teer ahs en-treh-gahs ee PRAH-zohs)

Let's brainstorm ideas and solutions.
Vamos fazer uma tempestade de ideias e soluções.
*(VAH-moosh fah-ZEHR OO-mah tem-peh-STAH-dee deh ee-DEY-ahs ee
soh-loo-SOHNS)*

We need to come up with a feasible plan.

Precisamos criar um plano viável.

(pre-see-MOHSH kree-AHR ooh PLAH-noh vee-AH-vehl)

Can we consider alternative options?

Podemos considerar opções alternativas?

(poh-DEH-moosh kohn-see-deh-RAR oh-PSOHNS al-tehr-NAH-tee-vahs)

Let's analyze the market trends and competition.

Vamos analisar as tendências de mercado e concorrência.

(VAH-moosh ah-nah-lee-ZAHR ahs ten-DEN-see-ahs deh mehR-CA-do ee kon-koh-REEN-see-ah)

We need to reach a compromise that satisfies both parties.

Precisamos chegar a um compromisso que satisfaça ambas as partes.

(pre-see-MOHSH cheh-GAHR ah oohm kom-proh-MEE-soh kee sah-tees-FAH-sah AM-bahs ahs PAHR-tes)

Can we negotiate the terms of the contract?

Podemos negociar os termos do contrato?

(poh-DEH-moosh ne-go-see-AHR ohs TEHR-mohs doh kon-TRAH-to)

Let's review the key points of the agreement.

Vamos revisar os pontos chave do acordo.

(VAH-moosh reh-VEE-zaHR ohs POYN-toosh KAY-deh doh ah-KWOHR-do)

We need to make sure that the deal is mutually beneficial.

Precisamos garantir que o acordo é benéfico para ambas as partes.

(pre-see-MOHSH gahr-an-TEER kee oh ah-KWOHR-doh eh beh-NEH-fee-ko PAH-rah AM-bahs ahs PAHR-tes)

Can we discuss the terms of payment in detail?

Podemos discutir os termos de pagamento em detalhes?

(poh-DEH-moosh dees-KOO-teer ohs TEHR-mohs deh pah-gah-MEN-too em deh-TA-lyis)

We need to find a solution that meets everyone's needs.
Precisamos encontrar uma solução que atenda às necessidades de todos.
(pre-see-MOHSH en-kohn-TRAHR ooh-mah soh-loo-SOHNG kee ah-TEN-dah ah neh-seh-SEE-dah-deh TOH-dohs)

Can we discuss the pricing and costs involved?
Podemos discutir os preços e custos envolvidos?
(poh-DEH-moosh dees-KOO-teer ohs PREH-soosh ee KOOS-toosh en-vohl-VEE-dohs)

Let's consider the risks and benefits of the deal.
Vamos considerar os riscos e benefícios do acordo.
(VAH-moosh kohn-see-deh-RAR ohs REES-kohs ee beh-neh-FEE-see-ohs doh ah-KWOHR-doh)

We need to establish clear communication channels.
Precisamos estabelecer canais de comunicação claros.
(pre-see-MOHSH ehs-tah-beh-LEH-sehr KAH-nah-eez deh ko-moo-nee-kah-see-own KLAH-rohsh)

Can we negotiate a better deal than the current one?
Podemos negociar um acordo melhor do que o atual?
(poh-DEH-moosh ne-go-see-AHR oom ah-KWOHR-doh MEH-lor doh kee ooh-AH-too)

Let's discuss the timeline and milestones of the project.
Vamos discutir o cronograma e marcos do projeto.
(VAH-moosh dees-KOO-teer o kroh-noh-GRAH-mah ee MAR-kohs doh proh-JEH-toh)

We need to make sure that all parties understand the terms and conditions.
Precisamos garantir que todas as partes entendam os termos e condições.
(pre-see-MOHSH gahr-an-TEER kee TOH-dahs ahs PAHR-tes ehn-tehn-DAHM ohs TEHR-mohs ee kohn-dee-SOHNS)

Can we explore different options before making a decision?
Podemos explorar diferentes opções antes de tomar uma decisão?
(poh-DEH-moosh eks-ploh-RAR dee-feh-REN-tehz oh-PSOHNS AHN-tehz deh toh-MAHR ooh-mah deh-see-ZAO)

Let's come up with a creative and innovative solution.
Vamos encontrar uma solução criativa e inovadora.
(VAH-moosh en-kohn-TRAHR ooh-mah soh-loo-SOHNG kree-AH-tee-vah ee ee-noh-vah-DOH-rah)

We need to find a way to make the deal work for everyone.
Precisamos encontrar uma maneira de fazer o acordo funcionar para todos.
(pre-see-MOHSH en-kohn-TRAHR ooh-mah mah-NEH-rah deh FAH-zer oh ah-KWOHR-doh foon-see-o-NAHR PAH-rah TOH-dohs)

Can we negotiate a more flexible agreement?
Podemos negociar um acordo mais flexível?
(poh-DEH-moosh ne-go-see-AHR oom ah-KWOHR-doh mah-eez fleh-KSEE-vehl)

Let's consider the long-term implications of this deal.
Vamos considerar as implicações de longo prazo desse acordo.
(VAH-moosh kohn-see-deh-RAR ahs eem-plee-kah-SOHNS deh LOHN-goh PRAH-zoh DEH-see ah-KWOHR-doh)

We need to make sure that both parties benefit from the deal.
Precisamos garantir que ambas as partes se beneficiem com o acordo.
(pre-see-MOHSH gahr-an-TEER kee ahm-BAHS ahs PAHR-tes see beh-neh-fee-SEE-ohm kohm oh ah-KWOHR-doh)

Can we negotiate a win-win situation?
Podemos negociar uma situação ganha-ganha?
(poh-DEH-moosh ne-go-see-AHR oom-ah see-too-ah-SOHNG GAHN-yah-GAHN-yah)

Let's find a solution that is mutually beneficial.
Vamos encontrar uma solução que seja mutuamente benéfica.
(VAH-moosh en-kohn-TRAHR ooh-mah soh-loo-SOHNG keh SEH-jah moo-too-AH-men-teh beh-NEH-fee-ka)

We need to make sure that all legal requirements are met.
Precisamos garantir que todos os requisitos legais sejam cumpridos.
(pre-see-MOHSH gahr-an-TEER kee TOH-dohs oh reh-kee-zee-tohsh leh-GAIS see-jahm koom-PREE-dohs)

Can we explore alternative solutions?
Podemos explorar soluções alternativas?
(poh-DEH-moosh eks-ploh-RAR soh-loo-SOHNGS ahl-ter-NAH-tee-vahs)

Let's make sure that the agreement is mutually beneficial.
Vamos garantir que o acordo seja mutuamente benéfico.
(VAH-moosh gahr-an-TEER kee oh ah-KWOHR-doh SEE-jah moo-too-AH-men-teh beh-NEH-fee-koh)

We need to be transparent and honest in our negotiations.
Precisamos ser transparentes e honestos em nossas negociações.
(pre-see-MOHSH sehr trahn-spa-REN-tehs ee oh-NEH-stohs ehm NOH-sahs neh-go-see-ah-SOHNS)

Can we come up with a compromise that satisfies both parties?
Podemos chegar a um compromisso que satisfaça ambas as partes?
(poh-DEH-moosh cheh-GAHR ah oom kohm-proh-MEE-soh kee sah-tee-SFAH ahm-BAHS ahs PAHR-tes)

We need to ensure that the agreement is feasible and realistic.
Precisamos garantir que o acordo seja viável e realista.
(pre-see-MOHSH gahr-an-TEER kee oh ah-KWOHR-doh SEE-jah vee-AH-vehl ee hee-AH-lee-stah)

Can we discuss the terms and conditions in more detail?
Podemos discutir os termos e condições com mais detalhes?
(poh-DEH-moosh dees-koo-TEER ohs TEHR-mohsh ee koh-dee-SOHNS kohm mah-eez deh-TAH-lyehsh)

Let's try to find a solution that satisfies both parties.
Vamos tentar encontrar uma solução que satisfaça ambas as partes.
(VAH-moosh TEHN-tahr ehn-kohn-TRAHR ooh-mah soh-loo-SOHNG keh sah-tee-SFAH ahm-BAHS ahs PAHR-tes)

We need to ensure that the agreement is fair and equitable.
Precisamos garantir que o acordo seja justo e equitativo.
(pre-see-MOHSH gahr-an-TEER kee oh ah-KWOHR-doh SEE-jah JUHS-too ee eh-kee-TEE-veh-toh)

Can we explore some alternative options?
Podemos explorar algumas opções alternativas?
(poh-DEH-moosh ehks-ploh-RAR ooh-mahsh ohp-SOHNS ahl-tehr-NAH-tee-vahs)

Let's review the proposal and come back with any questions or concerns.
Vamos revisar a proposta e voltar com quaisquer perguntas ou preocupações.
(VAH-moosh reh-VEE-zahr ah proh-POHS-tah ee VOHL-tahr kohm KWAYSS-kehr pehr-GOON-tahs oh pree-oh-koh-PAH-sohns)

What are the non-negotiable terms for your company?
Quais são os termos não negociáveis para sua empresa?
(KWYS sah-o os TEHR-mohsh NAOH nee-goh-see-AH-veh-ees pah-rah SOO-ah ehm-PREH-zah)

We are open to discussing different terms if it helps us reach a mutually beneficial agreement.
Estamos abertos a discutir termos diferentes se isso nos ajudar a chegar a um acordo mutuamente benéfico.
(ehs-TOH-mohsh ah-BEHR-toosh ah dees-koo-TEER TEHR-mohsh dee-feh-REHN-tehs seh EE-soh nohs ah-zoo-JAHR ah cheh-GAHR ah oom ah-KWOHR-doh moo-too-AHM-teh be-NEH-fee-koh)

Let's find a way to make this deal work for both of us.
Vamos encontrar uma maneira de fazer esse negócio funcionar para ambos.
(VAH-moosh ehn-kohn-TRAHR oo-mah mah-NEH-rah deh fah-ZEHR EH-seh neh-GOH-see-oh foon-see-oh-NAHR pah-rah ahm-BOHNS)

I think we're getting close to a mutually beneficial agreement.
Acho que estamos chegando perto de um acordo mutuamente benéfico.
(AH-shoh keh ehs-TAH-mohs cheh-GAHN-doh PEHR-toh deh oom ah-KWOHR-doh moo-too-AHM-teh be-NEH-fee-koh)

Can you provide some more information on the timeline for this project?
Você pode fornecer mais informações sobre o cronograma para este projeto?
(voh-SEH poh-deh fohr-neh-SEHR mahysh een-fohr-mah-SEE-ohns oh-bree kroh-noh-GRAH-mah pah-rah EH-steh proh-JEH-toh)

Printed in Great Britain
by Amazon

29662815R00119